Getting the Buggers to Add Up

Also available in the *Getting the Buggers* series

Getting the Buggers Excited about ICT, Karen Anderson
Getting the Buggers to Behave (4th edition), Sue Cowley
Getting the Buggers to Learn (2nd edition), Duncan Grey
Getting the Buggers to Think (2nd edition), Sue Cowley
Getting the Buggers to Write (3rd edition), Sue Cowley

Also available from Continuum

100+ Ideas for Teaching Mathematics, Mike Ollerton
The Mathematics Teacher's Handbook, Mike Ollerton
Resources for Teaching Mathematics 11–14, Colin Foster
Resources for Teaching Mathematics 14–16, Colin Foster

Getting the Buggers to Add Up

Third edition

MIKE OLLERTON AND PETER SYKES

Getting the Buggers

continuum

Continuum International Publishing Group

The Tower Building	80 Maiden Lane
11 York Road	Suite 704
London	New York
SE1 7NX	NY 10038

www.continuumbooks.com

British Library Cataloguing-in-Publication Data
A catalogue record for this book is available from the British Library.

ISBN: 978-1-4411-2239-1 (paperback)

Library of Congress Cataloging-in-Publication Data
Ollerton, Mike.
Getting the buggers to add up / Mike Ollerton and Peter Sykes. -- 3rd ed.
p. cm.
Includes bibliographical references and index.
ISBN 978-1-4411-2239-1 (pbk.) -- ISBN 978-1-4411-8086-5 (ebook (epub)) -- ISBN 978-1-4411-1395-5 (ebook (pdf)) 1. Mathematics--Study and teaching--Great Britain. I. Sykes, Peter. II. Title.
QA135.6.O55 2012
510.71′041--dc23

2011029896

Typeset by Fakenham Prepress Solutions, Fakenham, Norfolk NR21 8NN
Printed and bound in India

Contents

Contents

Part 4

Preface

When I was asked if I would be interested in writing a third edition of *Getting the Buggers to Add Up* my first response was 'Thank you, but no thank you.' As a freelancer who no longer teaches in my own classroom on a regular basis, I felt I may be out of touch with some of the new developments that teachers have to engage with. However, Mel Wilson from Continuum suggested I co-wrote the third edition with someone whom I felt might wish to join me on this venture. So I approached Peter Sykes, who I have known for almost 20 years. Peter is currently a Head of Faculty in a 1000+ 11–18 comprehensive and he was pleased to be involved. With Peter on board to offer his expertise as a practising secondary school teacher and head of faculty, things changed.

This edition, therefore, has been written by Peter and me. While the first and second editions described my personal journey through the elaborate maze of teaching, there being two authors with two personal journeys (despite sharing the same broad pedagogy) has rendered the word 'I' problematic in this new co-written edition. So, throughout the book 'I' refers to my own words and Peter's contributions appear in italics. Many of these are anecdotes relating Peter's experiences both in and outside the classroom. In response, I offer meta-commentaries, which Peter and I have discussed and agreed.

Many of you may already be familiar with my work and philosophy, so I would like to take this opportunity to introduce Peter Sykes as the co-author of this third edition. I have known Peter since 1993 when, as a 'mature' student, he re-trained to become a secondary mathematics teacher after a successful though foreshortened career in the mining industry. I was seconded one day a week from my role as Head of Mathematics at a school in Telford to St Martin's College, Lancaster and Peter was in one of the PGCE groups I worked with.

Professionally, Peter had a hunger for gathering as many ideas for the classroom as possible, and he was one of two of the students who regularly attended voluntary lunchtime sessions where we discussed such ideas. He is currently heading up his second mathematics department having worked as an advanced skills teacher (AST) before that.

In order to demonstrate how Peter 'ticks' as a mathematics teacher, below are nine words he feels encapsulates his practice: engaging, watching, discussing, questioning, listening, sharing, praising, assessing and laughing.

Engaging

I seek to use engaging activities to stimulate interest. These may be practical, problem-solving activities, using ICT such as spreadsheets or Logo, offering real-life situations such as working with plans and elevations from planning applications. For example, I use a planning application I submitted to the local council to build a garage showing front, side and plan views of the building. I usually lead a general discussion about why planning laws exist and often there are several students who have experienced this for themselves and make useful contributions. This generates interest from other students. In addition to giving a real-life context to the lesson, the drawings also include at least two scales: a site map and detailed drawings of the building. All applications are available from local council websites. I also try to engage groups of students by being enthusiastic about my subject at all times; when they enter my classroom or when I see them in the corridors between lessons, at break or lunchtime. Obviously, for effective learning to take place students need to be engaged in their work, so I rarely sit down behind the teacher's desk – I spend a lot of time circulating the room supporting and monitoring learning.

Watching

Sometimes I sit down in a classroom, at the back or at the side of the class. This creates an opportunity to watch the students at work and lets me see who is on or off task. It also reveals students' different approaches to learning. There are those who work in a self-contained way, some who converse with their neighbours about their work, some students persevere when faced with a problem while others immediately look for support. Just 30 seconds of uninterrupted watching provides fascinating insights into how learning takes place.

Discussing

In my classroom a student will occasionally announce: 'He's got that look on his face – he's not going to tell us.' They are, of course, referring to an unspoken declaration on my behalf when two or more students have made contributions to a whole-class discussion. There may be a difference of opinion about how to solve a problem or a disagreement on a mathematical process or even different suggestions, all of which are mathematically sound. An example of this occurred when reviewing the area of 2D shapes in preparation for further work about calculating the volume of prisms. The area of a rectangle posed no problems, but the area of a triangle produced the following discussion beginning with finding the area of a right-angled triangle:

Danny   I remember how to do this – you draw a rectangle using the triangle and calculate the area by multiplying the width and height of the rectangle and then dividing by two because the triangle is half the area of the rectangle.

The next triangle was scalene and Catherine made this contribution.

Catherine   You do the same thing by drawing a rectangle around the triangle, calculate the area of the rectangle but this time you divide by three because you have

	made three triangles and you just want the area of one of them.
Danny	No, that's not right – you still only divide by two.
Catherine	But there were just two triangles in the first example and we divided by two. Now there are three triangles so we divide by three.

Although Catherine's statement was incorrect, there was some logic to her argument. At this point I asked for other students to make and justify their own choice rather than me as teacher passing judgement. The students' understanding of the situation was resolved by another student drawing in the perpendicular height of the scalene triangle, thereby creating four triangles but clearly demonstrating that the area of the triangle was half the area of the rectangle, so dividing by two gave the correct answer.

Students tend to want to know who is right or wrong and expect me as their teacher to be the judge. I often deliberately refuse to make a decision. The key issue is that if I step in too early during such discussions then the students may, in future, wait for me to provide them with an 'answer'. However, by strategically holding back, my experience tells me that students will choose offer their ideas and discuss alternative suggestions, thus allowing more time for discussion and developing ideas; allowing other students to make contributions and make their own decisions. Apparently, I have a particular facial expression in these situations that some students recognise and realise that they are going to have to work a little harder on their own or as a group in order to make progress.

Questioning

Like so many activities in a classroom, this is a multi-directional activity – questioning should be taking place between the teacher and students, between students and the teacher and finally between student and student. It is also closely linked with the previous activity of discussing mathematics in the classroom. Using open rather than closed questions helps to generate discussions and I always emphasise how every student in my class should feel confident about asking any question at any time. I always work on the assumption that students ask questions because they need some clarification or guidance rather than it being a time-wasting activity. So even if the question appears 'trivial' it deserves to be answered positively rather than dismissively. One Year 10 student said to me that she couldn't believe how much patience I had answering student questions, but I pointed out that this was my job and answering questions is just as important as asking them.

Listening

This is a crucial skill in the development of students' understanding, and I am not simply referring to them listening to the teacher! During the many lesson observations I have carried out across different subjects, I have seen teachers ask a question and then, because the answer given by a student doesn't match the answer the teacher wants, he or she ignores the response and ask another student and then another until the 'right' answer is given. During this time, the teacher has stopped listening to perfectly valid alternative solutions and other possible avenues of development and as such the teacher is missing out on what the students are saying and ignoring vital clues about what students actually understand or potentially misconceive. Every answer needs to be carefully listened to and responded to, even if that means telling a student he or she is wrong. This respect for students' comments helps to develop a classroom environment where positive learning experiences take place.

Sharing

It is important for students to come to know and learn to use correct mathematical vocabulary; to recognise there is a vocabulary unique to mathematics. However, there are many occasions where my definition of a word or explanation of a concept can make things even more complicated and often a student will describe something in his or her own words more elegantly and simply. At these moments I like the student to share such an explanation with the whole class and give temporary ownership of the knowledge to the student. An example of this involved working with a Year 11 class on Pythagoras' Theorem. Having set up an activity for the students to 'discover' Pythagoras' Theorem, Carla explained to the whole class that the area of the largest square is calculated by adding together the area of the two smaller squares. For the next phase of the lesson I constantly referred to this as Carla's Rule as we calculated the areas of squares on right-angled triangles. Eventually, I explained that Pythagoras had also made the same connection over 2000 years ago. However, for that moment in that lesson Carla shared her ideas with everyone else and we shared in her success.

Praising

Telling the buggers when they have done well! Everyone feels better for a pat on the back and I try to do this individually in a quiet moment either during or after a lesson or collectively at the end. Praise, however, also needs to be tempered: too much too frequently or too readily can lessen its impact. Students certainly dislike being patronised, and over-exuberant praise can cause this – teaching is all about balance, about context and relationships.

Assessing

Assessment is an area where modern teaching jargon and a plethora of associated acronyms can result in experienced practitioners convincing themselves that they fail to adequately assess the progress of students' learning in their classrooms. However, when we strip down the language and put it in simple terms, we recognise that teachers are constantly monitoring and assessing students' progress and achievements; often unconsciously as a natural part of being a teacher. I apply assessment techniques during starter activities, when I am questioning students, during students' explanations, when I am carrying out in-class marking, during lesson recaps, when I respond to homework, etc. The big issue is what any teacher does with this massive amount of data … much more on that later in the book.

Laughing

I am sure there is laughter on at least one occasion during any of my lessons. This laughter is not achieved by telling jokes but by creating a positive learning environment where students feel safe and secure. As a result of the many conversations between me and students during a lesson there is always at least one situation that is amusing and generates laughter. For example, one day a student had not arrived to the lesson and I asked her working partner, 'Where's your sidekick?' Having misheard my question, she replied, 'I'm not psychic, it's you who's Psychic Sykes.' I replied, 'I knew you were going to say that.' There was a slight pause followed by a mirthful recognition of what I had said. The 'cornier' the better, I reckon!

PART 1

Introduction

Learners make sense of mathematics when they see for themselves what is 'going on' as they engage with concepts. Seeing something for oneself may or may not require a teacher to be present – in some instances sense-making occurs because a teacher is *not* present. However, this book has not been written to demean or to marginalise the role teachers have to play in supporting learning. It has been written to consider ways in which a teacher might seek to enable learners to engage in mathematical thinking so they learn to make sense of mathematics and discover what is going on. The following quote by Gattegno provides us with much to think about:

All I must do is to present [learners] with a situation so elementary that they all master it from the outset, and so fertile that they will all find a great deal to get out of it. (1963, 63)

I have reproduced the quote from Gattegno because, in part, it challenges the view of teaching being about 'passing on knowledge'. More importantly, the quote encourages us to reconsider what it means 'to teach'. Finding 'elementary' situations that are 'fertile' with possibilities for development, for students' mathematical enrichment, requires teachers to consider what underpins the mathematical concepts with which we intend our students to engage. This involves planning lessons that require us to go back to our own basic understanding of the mathematics we intend our students to work on. For example, if we want students to understand the concept of addition, we need to be clear in our own minds what it means to add two 'things' together. Similarly, for students to understand concepts such as multiplication, working out the area of a shape, Pythagoras' Theorem or calculus, we need to offer tasks that will enable students to construct their understandings of such concepts; constructivism being fundamental to sense-making.

There is a lovely card game produced by the Association of Teachers of Mathematics (ATM) called Fourbidden. One person takes a card and has to try to describe the word written on left-hand side of that card, e.g. 'Hexagon', without saying four further words – in this case 'sides', 'six', 'shape', 'bees' – that are written on the right-hand side of the card. I mention this in order to pose a couple of challenges. Firstly, how would you describe the process of 'addition' without using words such as 'total', 'plus', 'subtract' or 'combine'? Secondly, how would you describe the concept of 'area' using whatever words you like? My reason for posing these two challenges is to try to demonstrate that even the so-called easiest of concepts are not at all easy to describe and even less easy for a class of 30 individuals to understand. As such, a key aspect of sense-making is for learners to have first-hand experiences through which they construct meaning. This is in contrast to listening to a teacher's explanation or instructions followed by repeatedly practising a given method. Subsequently, for this introduction to the third edition of *Getting the Buggers to Add Up* I offer three thoughts. These are:

1 Teaching mathematics is complex.
2 Teaching does not necessarily equal learning.
3 Making sense of how anyone learns is even more complex.

Thought 1

Seeking to unravel and make sense of the complexity of teaching mathematics, finding the joys and meeting the challenges is largely what this book is about. Indeed, it is only when we accept the complexity of life in the classroom, when we realise there are no quick fixes or formulaic, step-by-step ways of organising our approaches to teaching, that we can stop looking for 'the' way to teach mathematics and instead look elsewhere at what it means to be a mathematics teacher.

Thought 2

There is often a misconstrued belief that teaching = learning. If this were the case then we could do away with assessment on the basis that if a teacher has taught concepts *x*, *y* and *z* then the learners have learnt concepts *x*, *y* and *z*. However, we know from experience we often learn something not because someone has taught us but because we taught ourselves; indeed, we have sometimes learnt something in spite of a teacher. The implications of this are to redesign what it means 'to teach' and to consider what roles a mathematics teacher plays in order to facilitate learning.

Thought 3

Since the introduction of the National Curriculum in 1989 learning has been measured across the compulsory school age range on a scale. How students' achievements are mapped on to this scale is difficult enough. However, in recent times such has been the need to provide 'data' either for Ofsted, for local authorities and for some senior managers in schools that decimalised scales have appeared. So one student might be 'given' a level 5.2 and another may get a 6.7. The abject nonsense of such an approach to grading is the kind of approach to assessment being played out here.

Returning to the complexity of learning, it is worth doing some mathematics to act as a vehicle for the wider consideration of the complexities of teaching and learning mathematics. So, to get you thinking mathematically, here is a puzzle. The intention is for you to think about how you engaged with the task in order to analyse what learning took place. Later, one person's response to the problem is described.

> *Find a cuboid with integer length dimensions and a surface area of 100cm².*

Okay, have you come up with a solution? Have you found two solutions? Can you prove there are only two solutions? You might have some further questions. I certainly have:

✓ Did you use trial and improvement?
✓ Did you try to create a systematic approach?
✓ What has this puzzle got to do with teaching and learning mathematics?
✓ If you were to use this puzzle in your classroom, what might you have worked on with the students the previous lesson or two?
✓ What might you ask students to do next?
✓ Why might you use or choose not to use a puzzle such as this in your teaching?
✓ What other learning qualities would students need to develop in order to get to work on such a problem?

I have used this problem many times in the past and solutions had always, seemingly, been gained through trial and improvement. However, on a recent occasion when working with a group of secondary teaching assistants, one delegate, Paddy, devised a cunningly systematic approach. Her solution was based upon some earlier work the group had been doing about exploring the different surface areas of cuboids made from 24 linking cubes. Paddy therefore already knew how to determine the surface area of a cuboid in terms of $2(lw + lh + wh)$.

Paddy explained how she had simplified this formula to $lw + lh + wh = 50$. From this she worked out that two of the dimensions, e.g. w and h, had to be multiplied together and then this result needed to be subtracted from 50. The remaining amount of surface area, i.e. $50 - wh$, then had to be divisible by the sum of the original two dimensions.

For example, had Paddy chosen two of the dimensions as 2 and 3, she then explained her method using the following steps:

1 $2 \times 3 = 6$;
2 Take 6 away from 50 leaving 44;
3 If 44 is divisible by the total of $(2 + 3)$ then she has a solution.

In this example 44 is not divisible by (2 + 3), therefore she needed to explore no further this particular situation. The beauty of her method was that when 50 – *wh* is divisible by (*w* + *h*) the resulting answer provides the third dimension, i.e.

(50 – *wh*) ÷ (*w* + *h*).

Though Paddy's method still required some degree of trial and improvement, it was far quicker than the standard number-crunching routine using the surface area formula of a cuboid. I relate this anecdote because it captures key issues this book is about:

1 the value of problem-solving as a vehicle for mathematical thinking;
2 the importance of finding the balance between teaching and learning;
3 the importance of sense-making through exploration;
4 the pleasure of solving a problem;
5 the inanity of seeking to capture such thinking in an examination;
6 the joy of achievement.

Miracle workers

Given the ever-increasing complexity of teaching, the impact of information technology upon the way children communicate and see the world and the increasing politicisation of education per se, it is miraculous that so many classrooms are safe, orderly places. To achieve this teachers perform miracles on a daily basis, often without realising it. When teachers are supported by senior managers who encourage risk-taking and evermore creative approaches to teaching and learning, then schools become dynamic and fulfilling places in which to learn. In brief, teachers need to be supported to continue to be miracle workers.

To achieve daily miracles, teachers develop marvellous interpersonal communication skills. They build sound relationships and construct classroom environments where mutual respect exists. They devise whole ranges of strategies and ways of responding to the plethora of situations they face day by day. Interactions are unpredictable. Something happens and action has to be taken. There is no recipe or guidebook to tell teachers how to make on-the-spot decisions, to explain what to say, how to say it or how to act. There is no substitute for experience. However, experience alone is not a sufficient condition to guarantee development of expertise. Through an ability to reflect upon, make sense of and rationalise experience, teachers develop an inner strength required to make sense of the enormous complexity of being a teacher. Through experience, teachers learn how to take the heat out of situations, when to step in and when to stand aside. They learn to be strategic, when to notice explicitly what is going on and when to ignore certain other events. It is not mere luck, therefore, that the vast majority of classrooms are safe, supportive and respectful places where effective and affective learning occurs, based upon positive relationships and interesting ideas.

Education is constantly under the media spotlight and is used (and abused) by politicians as a vehicle for pursuing the vote-catching agenda. Teachers deal not only with all kinds of events and situations concerning students but also with colleagues, parents, inspectors and the uninvited wasp that flies in. Certain events and responses to them may be predictable, but many are not, and teachers often have to think fast and respond speedily. Much of what teachers do is on the move and of the moment and this requires the development of skills based upon intuition and decision-making. There are important parallels here with assessment and about the kinds of conditions that enable students to show the best they can do – conditions that are not necessarily sitting still doing a test. This book contains a chapter devoted to assessment, so more on that later.

The effectiveness of decisions teachers make are largely determined by the type of atmosphere they seek to create in classrooms and by what they learn from experience. Our experiences tells us that seeking to grab students' attention, to gain their interest and to act upon natural inquisitiveness by offering problems and puzzles are key aspects of constructing a positive classroom atmosphere. Recognising the crucial impact the atmosphere in a classroom has upon the quality of learning cannot be understated, and this is an issue permeating the whole of this book. However, before leaving this issue of classroom atmosphere, we offer the following thought about listing the key elements that frame or describe one's practice. Being explicit about this can be an incredibly valuable exercise, in a similar way to how Peter described his practice in nine keywords in the foreword. Recognising the importance of trust; of students taking responsibility; of teacher honesty; of one's idiosyncrasies, such as being slightly crazy; of the value of display work; and the way visitors are greeted are examples of the kind of elements integral to classroom atmosphere. The importance of creating classrooms based upon challenge and interest cannot be understated.

This book, therefore, is about teaching mathematics based upon the central tenet that everything is connected, or to quote Sotto (1995, 43): 'One has to learn how the whole thing hangs together.'

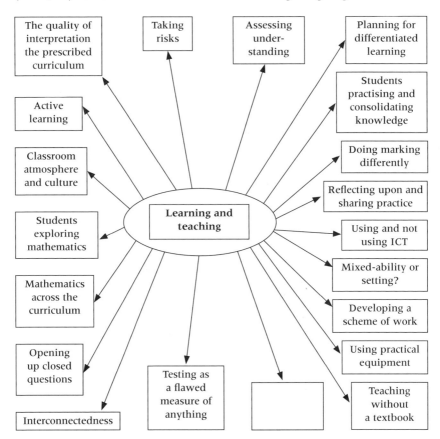

To this end we offer a spider diagram listing a range of issues that impact upon teaching and learning. The empty box at the bottom is to signify incompleteness, and readers might like to consider what issues you would add to or delete from this diagram. This diagram is not intended to be a comprehensive list, but it is a start. All the issues displayed are developed in this book. Some appear several times in different contexts, some have specific sections or chapters attributed to them.

The structure of this book

This book is written in four main parts. Part 1, including this introduction, explores the nature of mathematics and why anyone should wish to learn it. Part 2 is about contexts and ideas for classrooms together with some strategies and resources a teacher might use to support students' engagement with mathematics. Part 3 considers some of the wider issues that impact upon teachers and teaching mathematics. In Part 4 we fly a few kites and invite readers to consider the possibility and desirability of doing some things differently.

Throughout the book ideas are offered for possible use in mathematics classrooms. We are acutely aware of not wishing to offer 'tips for teachers'. However, there is nothing within these pages that Peter or I have not either used in our teaching or observed in other classrooms. The next section of this Introduction considers frameworks within which education is structured and controlled.

Who or what controls our teaching?

Ever since James Callaghan's Ruskin Lecture in 1976 education has been under the political spotlight, with an increased amount of political interference. To gain control over schools and teachers, successive governments have sought ways of prescribing not only the curriculum but also teaching and assessment methods, the latter mainly in the form of an antiquated and a thoroughly inadequate testing regime. A significant concern, therefore, for teaching, as a potentially fantastic profession, is the impact politics has upon what happens in schools and individual classrooms. At worst, the result is to reduce the teacher's role to that of 'compliant' technician, turning flair and creativity into a teaching-to-the-test mode. Such a political agenda reduces children's learning and their achievements to simplistic 'measurable' outcomes dressed up in the clothes of 'standards'. This, in turn, requires quantifiable data to provide information for publication in the form of league tables. Such reductionist forces may find favour in a Gradgrindian (*Hard Times*, Charles Dickens) philosophy. However, it leaves these 21st-century citizens despairing over its limitations and its inadequacies. We must find ways of informing political and civil servants of the complexity of imposing structures and 'standards' in education in ways which fail to recognise that classrooms are emotional places. Learning cannot be reduced to a series of levels or grades monitored by tests and outside agencies.

Examinations

The National Curriculum together with testing at 7, 11 and 14 emerged from the 1998 Education Reform Act. Add in GCSE at 16, and there has clearly been a massive amount of prescription and control over compulsory education via testing. Although testing at ages 7 and 14 has been replaced by teacher assessment, this is merely an indictment of the frailties of testing in the first instance. However, the pressure to test and, therefore, to teach-to-the-test at 11 and 16 prevails. If this was not damaging enough schools have, more recently, been presented with FACME. This is not a profanity, merely an acronym (Five A* to C grades including Mathematics and English) – an initiative bringing further pressure on teachers. Such pressure seeks to turn teachers of mathematics and English into GCSE examination machines and is yet another ill-thought-out, knee-jerk scheme dreamt up by politicians in a bid to gather spurious information to demonstrate that their policies are 'working'. Sadly, it is such schemes that directly undermine how students develop as mathematicians. However, all is not lost! FACME will soon be integrated into or replaced by the 'English Bac', thus creating more prescription. Exactly where this leaves Year 9 students' options is anybody's guess. However did we arrive at such an impasse?

Of greater importance is how teachers balance the pressure of teaching-to-the-test against teaching for depth of understanding. To develop students' mathematical capabilities we recognise

11

that to function mathematically far transcends what can be tested. Processes such as pattern spotting, conjecturing, generalising, proving and how such processes are communicated are fundamental to students' development. This book, therefore, is also about teachers' central sphere of influence; what we are constantly capable of making an impression upon – our classroom and the students who come through the door. Although we cannot ignore the impact national policies have upon schools, we can do something that effective teachers have done since time immemorial – quietly and confidently to subvert the politicising nonsense and pay attention to what really matters. Learning.

Here is a simple problem, perhaps a 'rich task' that can reveal much about students' mathematical capabilities, none of which could be adequately assessed in a test:

Cut out these three shapes and make new shapes by fitting edges together of the same length.

A starting question is:
How many different shapes can be made?
A range of possible developmental questions are:
How many sides does each of your shapes have?
What are the names of the shapes you have made?
Can you find any more shapes? This could lead to the development of a system.
Why do you think you have found them all? This could lead to a possible proof.
How might the shapes be sorted or classified? This could lead to the construction of Carroll or Venn diagrams, e.g. four-sided shapes and shapes with right angles.

Which of your shapes contain only line symmetry?
Which of your shapes contain only rotational symmetry?
Which of your shapes have both line and rotational symmetry?
What are the angles inside each shape? This could lead to summing angles within the different shapes to emerge.
Can you make a tiling design from one of your more interesting shapes?

Harder questions could be based upon finding the perimeters of the shapes, perhaps by denoting the lengths of the sides of one of the smaller triangles a (the shorter side) and b (the longer side).

This trapezium has a perimeter of $4a + b$.

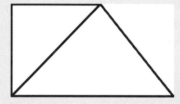

This, of course, is an example of 'collecting like terms'. However, you may prefer to use the symbols s (for shortest side) and l (for the longer side), as pupils could begin by writing the perimeter of the trapezium above as, short + short + two shorts + long or four short sides and one long side.

As the task stands, there are opportunities for pupils to think about the areas of the shapes in terms of fractional amounts. Again referring to the trapezium, its area would be 3/4 of the original square. If we now draw in a further dissection line by halving one of the smaller triangles, we now have a configuration of shapes with relative areas of 1/2, 1/4, and two with an area of 1/8.

Assessment is inextricably linked to effective teaching and learning, and when wider forms of formative and summative assessment are encouraged, teachers become confident to work in more creative ways. Teachers' professionalism must be recognised and this can be achieved through the responsibility they, and students, are given for assessing achievement. Fortunately, the Assessment for Learning agenda is becoming recognised as a potentially powerful way of supporting students' learning, and we develop this in Chapter 11.

Throughout this book we offer a wide number of ideas based upon practice. Of course, many of these ideas will already be in use in many classrooms. Others, however, may be relatively new or currently unused and may have potential for being incorporated into schemes of work undergoing development. We are conscious, however, that any idea is only as good as the intention behind the person wanting to use it. We do not, therefore, seek to prescribe ways of teaching. Instead, we offer 45 years worth of collective experience in classrooms that we hope readers will be able to consider and potentially adapt into practice.

Anybody reading this book could easily think 'Well, yes, in an ideal world ...' However, nobody inhabits an ideal world. Utopia does not exist and it is certainly not worth waiting around for someone else – a head of department, a headteacher, an advisor or a politician – to change things for us. The only people who can create change in our classroom are ourselves.

Getting the Buggers to Add Up therefore is an attempt to offer alternative visions and different ways of teaching mathematics. For some, the book may serve to strengthen and consolidate their beliefs about teaching mathematics. Others may have different, more adverse reactions. One or two politicians or civil servants may dip into the book and consider the policies that drive the teaching of mathematics and think 'I wonder if these tests really are driving down standards ...?' Whosoever reads this book, I hope there is something within the pages that will have some small impact upon pedagogy.

Developing a pedagogy

A fundamentally important issue for any teacher to engage with is to find the balance between achieving personal and professional autonomy and resisting prescription emanating from top-down autocracy and overzealous bureaucracy. We can achieve the former and resist the latter by developing our pedagogy, by considering what we believe to be important. This involves rationalising how we most effectively teach while at the same time revealing our values. The issue of values-in-action is developed in my *Creating Positive Classrooms* (2003). In the mathematics classroom we seek to achieve this by carefully considering how we want our students to experience mathematics:

✓ Through enquiry based upon problem-posing and problem-solving.
✓ By experiencing a range of strategies.
✓ Through the use of a wide range of resources to provide first-hand engagement with concepts.
✓ By experiencing different ways of assessing achievement.
✓ Through 'pure' mathematics where structures, relations, connections, logic and the complexity of mathematics are explored, for example:

> **Create a data set which has a mode of 3, a median of 4 and a mean of 5.**

✓ Further approaches are through cross-curricular and functional situations where students have opportunities to see how mathematics both models and helps to make sense of natural, physical, sociological and economic environments. A simple example of this would be to ask students to collect data from home, for example:

> **Find out how many household tasks are carried out in a typical week at home.**

Students can subsequently work on questions such as:
- How much time does each task take?
- Who does them?
- What proportion of the time taken for tasks done at home is carried out by different people?
- How could this information be represented pictorially?

– What are the implications of your findings?
– Can data from different students' households be compared?

These ways of working are within the tradition of problem-posing and problem-solving and require us to find ways of reducing our didactic mode of teaching and increasing exploratory approaches to learning.

Developing a pedagogy based upon problem-posing and problem-solving to support learning is a recurrent theme throughout this book, and as such it is worth asking what a problem-posing/problem-solving mathematics curriculum looks like. To begin to answer this question it may be useful to consider what such a curriculum would *not* look like. It would not look like students being asked to provide answers to exercises from textbooks. This is because the overuse of textbooks is anti-educational on a number of fronts, such as:

✓ they are trivial and fail to provide students with purposeful problems to solve
✓ they do not deepen students' conceptual development;
✓ they fail to help students make sense of the interconnected nature of mathematics;
✓ they can occupy a great deal of students' time with little to show for their endeavours;
✓ they are boring both for students to do and for teachers to mark!

Typically, textbook questions are based upon practising specific narrow skills, such as: 'Round the following to two places of decimal: a) 0.61532 b) 3.7891 c) 23.0237'. While some students may answer such questions correctly, this approach does not help students understand when it is useful to round a result of a calculation to a certain degree of accuracy. Neither does it help students transfer their learning from one situation to another (and frequently from one lesson to another).

Apologies if this next statement sounds rather obvious, but here goes. A problem-posing, problem-solving curriculum or scheme of work is based upon posing and solving problems. The key issue is to find wide-ranging problems worth posing and to determine how to fit such problems into coherent, structured schemes of work.

There are thousands of problems within the domain of school mathematics and we do not need to look much further than the following sources:

✓ The Association of Teachers of Mathematics (ATM)
✓ The Mathematical Association
✓ The National Centre for Excellence in the Teaching of Mathematics
✓ The Nrich maths project (University of Cambridge)
✓ The Shell Centre (University of Nottingham)

These sources, together with a few books from fantastic authors such as Martin Gardner, David Wells, Doug French and Brian Bolt, not forgetting Henry Ernest Dudeney, will stock up any scheme of work for evermore.

To conclude this introduction, here are a couple of problems you might like to contemplate:

> *Choose a whole number between 10 and 20.*
> *Think of this number as the perimeter (P) of a triangle whose sides are integer length.*
> *Construct one such triangle using a pencil, compasses and a straight edge.*
> *Consider what other (integer) lengths could form triangles with the same perimeter.*

Some follow-up tasks and questions are:

✓ Construct a system in order to be sure you have found all possible solutions.
✓ Explore different P values for number of possible triangles.
✓ Using a chosen P value, what are the areas of each triangle?
✓ What are the angles in each triangle?

Whilst the initial couple of tasks may be suitable for Year 6 to Year 8 students, the tasks about calculating area and angles would be more suited to Year 10 or Year 11 students. This is because the level of content involves Pythagoras, algebraic manipulation, solving a quadratic and trigonometry. Thus such a problem could be written into a late Key Stage 2/early Key Stage 3 scheme of work and subsequently be revisited at Key Stage 4.

A second problem that spans the age range from 5 to 16+ requires the use of a set of dominoes and is quite simple:

> **Without counting each spot one by one, find ways of working out the total number of spots in a set of dominoes.**

Of course, this could be simplified by using a smaller set of dominoes. Interestingly, the mapping from the set size to the number of spots is a cubic function. Again, determining where a problem such as this might best fit within a scheme of work is the main challenge.

Finally, from a pedagogic perspective, one of the most important features of offering students problems to work on is the surprises that can occur and the joy of seeing students come up with their own methods and solutions. I recently offered this problem to a group of teachers attending a Mathematics Specialist Teacher (MaST) conference in Manchester, though instead of using a 6-6 set of I distributed small 3-3 sets of card-laminated dominoes. After a few minutes three solutions were forthcoming:

Solution 1 In a 3-3 set there are five 3s, five 2s, five 1s and five 0s. By carrying out the calculation $(3 + 2 + 1 + 0) \times 5$ we get the answer 30.

Solution 2 In a 3-3 set there are five pairs of dominoes whose spot total each time is six, i.e. 3-3 with 0-0, 3-2 with 0-1, etc., so $6 \times 5 = 30$.

Solution 3 Altogether on the 10 dominoes there are 20 spaces. The values 0, 1, 2 and 3 are equally distributed among these 20 spaces. If we take the average of $0 + 1 + 2 + 3$ we gain

1.5. Multiplying by the number of spaces by the average gives the total, i.e. 1.5 × 20 = 30.

It is our hope that anyone who reads this book will feel encouraged to take risks, to try out new ideas, but most of all to consider the impact of the ways we teach upon those we have responsibility for teaching.

1

What is mathematics, why teach it and why learn it?

Mathematics is beautiful, intriguing, elegant, logical, amazing and mind-blowing; a language and a set of systems and structures used to make sense of and describe the physical and natural world. It is a set of tools and processes used in decision-making, a discipline upon which questions are formulated and problems are solved. It is used to model environmental conditions and applied to make sense of social phenomena. Mathematics can help build bridges and bring food to the hungry.

Mathematics is also frightening, boring, debilitating and can appear illogical; a thing many people made, or make, little sense of at school. It can be used to discriminate and separate children into those who can and those who cannot, those who do and those who do not understand, and, as a consequence, mathematics can serve to undermine many individuals' confidence as learners. Mathematics can be used to create weapons of war and destroy the economic and social fabric of societies.

The degree to which an individual perceives mathematics in positive or negative ways will largely be determined by the ways in which it is experienced at school and in the home. All disciplines are of equal value; they are often dependent upon one another and have infinite meeting points. However, mathematics holds a particularly interesting place in the curriculum as the subject that creates barriers and causes learners a deal of stress and anxiety. It is important, therefore, as teachers of mathematics, that we occasionally pause to reflect upon what we think mathematics is, to ask ourselves why we teach mathematics and consider what experiences we want students to have as they learn mathematics. It is similarly important that politicians, inspectors and educationalists who have key responsibilities for the way children's learning is 'measured' recognise the significant impact that methods of assessment have upon the way mathematics is taught and learnt.

What is the nature of mathematics?

To explore this question here are two quotes from sources written almost fifty years apart. The first is from Richard Courant and Herbert Robbins in their 1941 book *What is Mathematics?*

Mathematics as an expression of the human mind reflects the active will, the contemplative reason and the desire for aesthetic perfection. Its basic elements are logic and intuition, analysis and construction, generality and individuality.

The second is from *Non-Statutory Guidance*, a National Curriculum Council publication (1989, 2.5):

Mathematics is not only taught because it is useful. It should be a source of delight and wonder, offering pupils intellectual excitement and an appreciation of its essential creativity.

Reflecting upon my experiences as a learner, there was a lot of 'mechanical' arithmetic involved, and I did plenty of exercises. However, I was not taught about the puzzlement of mathematics; neither was I taught to appreciate its creative or aesthetic value. I subsequently recognise the value I now place upon education is related more to the way I was taught than what I was taught. In art lessons, for example, I was encouraged to make decisions and provided with choices about how to go about a task. This gave me a greater interest in learning than being 'made' to do countless exercises and pointless calculations and to apply seemingly useless formulae.

Recognising how I was taught and considering how I might teach, to provide students with access to the fascination of mathematics, is a paramount consideration. Fascination. Now there is an interesting word to associate with teaching and learning mathematics. More than a quarter of a century ago two of ten aims suggested by HMI for teaching mathematics were firstly awareness of the fascination of mathematics and secondly imagination, initiative and flexibility of mind in mathematics (1985, 3–4). Applying a criterion of 'fascination' to one's teaching is certainly an interesting challenge. The anecdote below relates to one of Peter's colleagues, Helen, who sought to make the concept of the volume of a cone a 'fascinating' one:

> *Halloween was approaching, so Helen bought half a dozen witches' hats and used laminate sheets to make conical inners that fitted into the hats. She then got the students to fill the hats with green jelly (liquid form) using measuring jugs so they knew what the volume was of each hat. During a previous lessons students had calculated the volume of prisms by multiplying the cross-sectional area by length (or height) so they knew they had to work out the area of the witch's hat at its widest point. They did this by drawing a circle of the same radius as the hat and counting squares. Having measured the perpendicular height of their hat and multiplied the two measures together to gain a volume, students began to notice the result was approximately three times greater than the volume of the jelly … If the students never remember the formula, I'm sure they will never forget the day they filled a witch's hat with green jelly!*

Of course, learning mathematics is not about memory alone. Learning mathematics is essentially about being able to construct ideas from first principles and applying this knowledge when a situation or a solution to a problem requires it. Understanding how to reconstruct a concept is of far greater value than trying to remember all kinds of formulae; however, once a formula becomes second nature learners can clearly problem-solve more efficiently.

This begs important questions about what any teacher thinks the nature of mathematics is, why we teach mathematics and how we encourage students to learn mathematics. Seeking to understand the nature of mathematics is also a useful precursor to deal with the kind of questions adolescents inevitably and quite understandably ask about why they need to learn mathematics. Trying to convince students about the value of learning trigonometry in order to determine where to stand when a tree falls down may provide mirth. However, it is unlikely to offer a sufficiently convincing justification about why they need to learn it. Yet stopping to think about what the nature of mathematics is can be unnerving, challenging, complex and illuminating.

Considering whether mathematics exists as a set of rules that individuals from different civilizations throughout time have 'discovered' or whether it is something that has been constructed and 'invented' to make sense of the world is a worthy area for discussion. Such questions can be posed to students and would sit comfortably in any mathematics classroom where exploration and discussion are encouraged. As busy teachers, however, who have tomorrow's lessons to plan, marking to do and reports to write, entertaining such thoughts for more than a short period of time may be a luxury we can rarely afford. Yet if our engagement with such ideas underpins what we do in mathematics classrooms and impacts in fundamental ways on how we teach mathematics it is important to dwell upon such questions.

Mathematics is a language for describing and giving meaning to natural and social phenomena a set of processes or ways of thinking in order to solve problems. These are the processes of:

- ✓ Sorting and ordering;
- ✓ Pattern spotting;
- ✓ Classifying;
- ✓ Interpreting;
- ✓ Evaluating;
- ✓ Hypothesising;
- ✓ Conjecturing;
- ✓ Generalising;
- ✓ Proving.

Problem-solving is a significant methodology in helping students learn mathematics. This is because mathematics is a set of inter-related systems and structures, connected in many different ways. Helping students see such links, to learn to connect ideas together, as well as understanding concepts themselves is central to sense-making.

So – why learn mathematics?

Some of the more debilitating questions students might ask any teacher are:

✓ 'Why are we doing this?'
✓ 'What's the point of learning all this stuff?'
✓ 'What use will this be to me when I leave school?'

Such questions might be construed as confrontational, especially if the teacher perceives they are asked in a particularly way, or if a student's timing has been 'inch-perfect' in terms of stopping the teacher when in full flow! Students are intelligent enough to realise that questions such as these provide good sport for testing out the teacher, or at least are a potential distraction from the lesson. On the other hand, such questions, perhaps asked in a more positive manner, might be a student's genuine desire to understand something, to go deeper into the mathematics. Whatever the reason, once a question has been posed it can be very difficult to ignore and seemingly impossible to answer in a way that is likely to placate the questioner.

Instead of seeking to offer glib answers to such questions, I intend to consider what a mathematics teacher might do to use such questions in a positive way and prevent them from turning a lesson into a difficult experience.

Pre-empting the inevitable and valuing openness

Asking a whole class a question such as: 'What do you think the point of learning mathematics is?' can be useful, perhaps at the beginning of a new academic year. Arranging the chairs in a ring and initially asking pairs of students to discuss this question for a minute or two before taking any responses is one possible strategy. Such a question can be posed to all ages of students ... sometimes I have received more coherent responses from 11 year olds than from undergraduates! I have asked such a question while a class is working on a particular topic. On other occasions it could posed as a homework task, to be picked up and discussed in the following lesson. Such an approach is intended to create an atmosphere of trust and openness where students' views are valued so they are encouraged to scrutinise, interrogate and evaluate mathematics. This may sound incredibly highfalutin and theoretical, yet, having taught thousands of adolescents, I find this approach particularly valuable. This is because it is a planned aspect of practice, designed to challenge students to question the value of mathematics for themselves. Bugger – this is beginning to read like 'tips for teachers', something I wish to avoid in this book. The big issue is about determining the kinds of attitudes and atmospheres we want in our classrooms. The beliefs we hold determine what goes on in our classrooms and how our students experience and make sense of mathematics. Examining our beliefs and deciding how we want the culture of our class-rooms to be, to look, to sound and to feel are personal decisions we choose or choose not to make. The remainder of this chapter focuses on ways we try to apply the issues raised above to school mathematics and ways of engaging children in mathematics in the classroom.

How do we learn mathematics?

What does it mean to learn mathematics? As discussed earlier, learning mathematics is in part about reconstructing knowledge and concepts from first principles. It is also about students seeing mathematics as an interconnected set of concepts. For example, learning how all the concepts involved in graphing a quadratic function of the form $ax^2 + bx + c$ (assuming they have previously worked confidently with coordinates and plotting and drawing linear functions) are connected together requires understanding the following:

✓ crossing points on the x-axis (if any exist);
✓ the crossing point on the y-axis;
✓ the turning point;
✓ the line of symmetry;
✓ factorisation;
✓ completing the square algorithm;
✓ the impact of changing the coefficients *a*, *b*, and *c*.

To cause students to make sense of all this information they need to be provided with opportunities to explore and discuss quadratics, turning points, crossing points, etc. Above all, they need to be given tasks so they process this information. Again, here it is our system of examinations that undermines effective learning. Giving students a formula to help them regurgitate the solutions to a quadratic equation may help them answer a question in an examination, but what have they learnt? Providing a correct or a desired response to a narrow question in a short period of time in a high-stakes examination is not going to create the environment for fascination or for deep learning. One of the more disturbing things students may learn is that mathematics is a load of gobbledygook.

This, in fact, was what an A level mathematics student alluded to several years ago. I was helping a neighbour to prepare for his AS examination. He was a diligent and highly capable student and we spent some evenings going through past papers. Towards the end of one session he turned to me and said, 'I hate maths, Mike!' His comment was neither intended nor received as a sign of his thanklessness for my help – it was a cry from the heart. He could jump through all the necessary hoops and he would go on to gain a grade A in the AS examination, yet he had little or no idea of the fundamental processes he needed to apply. Although this is but one anecdote about one highly capable mathematics student being turned off the subject, his story resonates with the kind of concerns raised by Professor Adrian Smith's enquiry into post-14 mathematics education, *Making Mathematics Count* (2004). In a letter to the Secretary of State for Education in the Foreword to the report, Smith wrote:

27

we have a curriculum and qualifications framework that fails to meet the mathematical requirement of learners, fails to meet the needs and expectations of higher education and employers and fails to motivate and encourage sufficient numbers of young people to continue with the study of mathematics post-16.

This must be something of a concern to everyone involved in mathematics education, especially as many recurring themes and concerns were raised 30 years ago in the Cockcroft Report. Learning mathematics is about constructing new knowledge and the role of the teacher is crucial in terms of how learners are helped to formulate their constructions. When knowledge is used and applied in problem-solving situations, concepts become assimilated into learners' existing knowledge. The issue of skills emerging though problem-solving resonates with the Cockcroft Report:

Mathematics lessons in secondary schools are often not about anything. You collect like terms or learn the laws of indices with no perception of why anyone needs to do such things. There is excessive preoccupation with a sequence of skills and quite inadequate opportunity to see the skills emerging from the solution of problems (1982, para. 462).

Learning mathematics is a mixture of conscious and unconscious competence; of students coming to know instinctively how to make sense of a problem; of being prepared to work hard on something when 'stuckness' stares them in the face.

Accelerated learning? How about deepening and decelerating learning instead?

I have become increasingly concerned over the notion of accelerated learning. My concern arises with the notion of students being rushed to engage with mathematical concepts at too early an age. The danger is of students being accelerated to get to the end of a mathematical journey at the expense of enjoying and making sense of the views on the way. To quote Robert Pirsig in *Zen and the Art of Motorcycle Maintenance*: 'To live only for some future goal is shallow. It's the sides of the mountain which sustain life, not the top' (1974, 199). One consequence of accelerated learning is that students miss out on the pleasure of seeing wider aspects of a mathematical journey in order to arrive somewhere at a faster rate than might be good for their deep conceptual development.

As an example, consider teaching Pythagoras' Theorem where an intended outcome is for students to memorise the formula: $a^2 + b^2 = c^2$. I have had some interesting experiences of working with Year 9 students where class teachers informed me they had just 'done' Pythagoras. However, upon posing a simple problem about working out the perimeters of triangles formed on a nine-pin geoboard, no student has ever suggested using Pythagoras: on one occasion it became abundantly clear the class had not experienced Pythagoras geometrically. Thus they could not relate the superscripts in the formula to areas of squares. They could chant the formula, but had little idea of what it meant or of its applications.

Learning Pythagoras' Theorem involves so much more than arriving at the formula, and I develop this later in the chapter. One way to gauge students' understanding of Pythagoras is to give pupils problems that require the application of the theorem, yet the problem itself does not immediately say 'use Pythagoras'. For example,

> On a 16-dot square grid (4-by-4 grid) draw a triangle with the longest perimeter.

Because the solution is a non right-angled triangle, using and applying Pythagoras' Theorem may not be immediately obvious. This means some students will have to dig into their mathematical toolkits and make consciously competent decisions to use Pythagoras to reach a solution. Other, perhaps more intuitive students, will use Pythagoras' Theorem as a matter of course. There will be other students who may not know where to start, in which case there is even less point in trying to accelerate them off on to something else.

This problem is ripe for development by posing e.g.

> *On an* n *by* n *dot grid determine the perimeter with the longest perimeter.*

The 'beauty' of this problem lies in the fact that a) Pythagoras' Theorem is omnipotent in reaching 'a' solution and b) there are two generalities to create, one when *n* is odd and one when *n* is even.

Whatever the scenario, the central issue is the need to help students construct new knowledge and to deepen their understanding from the basis of whatever their existing knowledge is. To achieve this, students need problems to solve that are initially accessible and ultimately challenging.

Learning mathematics through problem-solving

I base effective problem-solving approaches upon the following four planning criteria:

1 enabling access to all students;
2 providing a range of answers to be forthcoming;
3 catering for different paces of working;
4 posing different extension tasks.

A comment I have often heard in relation to using problems in mathematics classrooms is students must first learn a concept before they can use and apply this knowledge. I offer another perspective. This is to provide problems through which students begin to construct deeper knowledge about other, connected concepts. A simple example is based upon using the following problem:

> *In how many different ways can I multiply 2 whole numbers together to make 24?*

The spider diagram below is an attempt to show the various concepts such a seemingly innocuous question can open up.

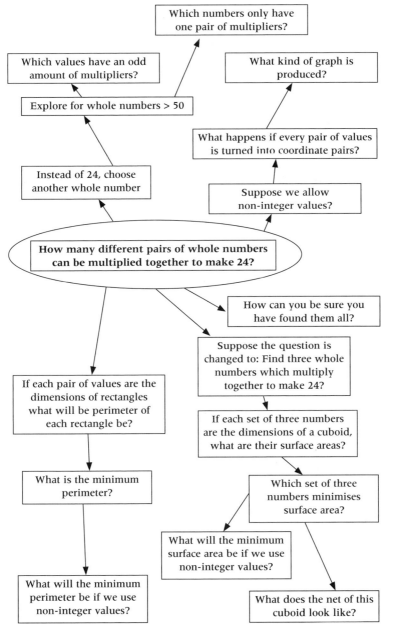

Which numbers only have one pair of multipliers?

Which values have an odd amount of multipliers?

What kind of graph is produced?

Explore for whole numbers > 50

What happens if every pair of values is turned into coordinate pairs?

Instead of 24, choose another whole number

Suppose we allow non-integer values?

How many different pairs of whole numbers can be multiplied together to make 24?

How can you be sure you have found them all?

Suppose the question is changed to: Find three whole numbers which multiply together to make 24?

If each pair of values are the dimensions of rectangles what will be perimeter of each rectangle be?

If each set of three numbers are the dimensions of a cuboid, what are their surface areas?

What is the minimum perimeter?

Which set of three numbers minimises surface area?

What will the minimum surface area be if we use non-integer values?

What will the minimum perimeter be if we use non-integer values?

What does the net of this cuboid look like?

The 'basic' concept upon which the ideas in spider diagram are based is that of multiplying whole numbers together. As above, this problem will serve as a practice and consolidation opportunity for some students whereas others will use their knowledge of divisors to work on other concepts, e.g.

✓ multiplication involving non-integer values;
✓ plotting coordinates;
✓ drawing graphs;
✓ properties of prime and square numbers;
✓ dimensions, nets and surface areas of cuboids;
✓ perimeters of rectangles of a fixed area;
✓ square roots.

Clearly, students in a class will be on different continuums, ranging from having little knowledge to being 'at home' with any of these concepts. As such, a key role of the teacher is to make decisions, based upon moment-by-moment interactions with students, to determine who is ready to move on to another task and who needs to stay with the initial starting task. Using problem-solving approaches therefore enables the teacher to cause students to develop their own interconnected knowledge webs. In broad terms, this is all part of the ongoing assessment mix … everything is connected.

Mathematics and creativity

Finding a definition of creativity within the context of teaching and learning mathematics is not easy. In the HMI report *Expecting the Unexpected: Developing Creativity in Primary and Secondary Schools* (2003) there are just three references, one of which raised a concern of teachers not letting go:

> *For some teachers, there is unwillingness, perhaps based on shaky subject knowledge, to let pupils find their own solution to problems. In mathematics, for example, pupils in some schools are taught standard computational methods first rather than finding ways of adding and subtracting for themselves.*

This questions the value of algorithmic-type teaching and instead focuses upon the importance of learning through greater self-determination. This can only emerge through exploration and by working on more open questions. In the same report an example of effective practice is described by a teacher posing the question: 'The answer is 25, so what is the question?'

Sadly, mathematics is not widely thought of as a creative discipline. Yet when creative mathematical thinking is encouraged, when questions open up different possibilities, students have opportunities to see for themselves that mathematics can be creative and not limited to right or wrong answers. In such circumstances students grow to believe they are capable of finding more than one answer to a problem or that there may be more than one way of carrying out a task. Consequently, students feel they have something to contribute, something worth saying. There are important principles here about enabling a wider range of students to participate in whole-class discussion. This requires the use of a far wider range of strategies than the commonly used 'hands-up' approach. To achieve this participation, greater use can be made of asking more open types of questions.

Asking more open-type questions

There are a plethora of questions and problems that can open up the possibility of students offering different answers and methods. How answers are accepted and what value is given to answers received are key aspects of practice based on asking open questions. A simple example for young children would be questions based upon something I call 'the five-ness of 5'.

The idea is to explore the existence of the number 5 both inside and outside the classroom; to find different ways and the different contexts where the number 5 appears, e.g.:

✓ Arrange 5 teddy bears in different ways.
✓ Find a number 5 in a set of dominoes. How many 5s are there?
✓ Find the number 5 in a pack of cards. How many 5s are there?
✓ If the teacher were to choose groups of 5 children, how

many girls and how many boys could there be in each group?

✓ How many groups of 5 children can be made from your class? Are there some children left over?

✓ Find a shape with 5 sides in your classroom.

✓ Make up 5 questions that you would really like to ask your teacher.

✓ Make up a story about the number 5.

✓ Find 5 tins of different kinds of food at home.

✓ Ask someone at home to say the 5 times table.

✓ Make a note of what you are doing at 5 o'clock tonight.

✓ What are your 5 favourite toys?

✓ Find 5 places where the number 5 is written somewhere at home.

At issue here, with regard to creativity, are:

1 young children being encouraged to make up their own questions;
2 some answers will be different, and this could lead to a discussion about these differences;
3 some outcomes will be the same, leading to sharing and checking.

The main purpose is to cause children to engage with the 'anything-ness of anything'; for them to see the same numerical amount in different contexts.

For older Key Stage 3 students a similar strategy could be used based upon, for example, 'the pi-ness of pi'. Students could be asked to find out about the number pi historically, arithmetically, geometrically and algebraically prior to a sequence of lessons about pi.

This means students have opportunities to arrive at a lesson with some knowledge of pi.

The beauty of the planning process lies in being able to apply it to many kinds of problems to provide students with access to all areas of the mathematics curriculum. This process is developmental, in terms of students working on ideas that underpin and extend conceptual understanding.

Ideas offered so far in this chapter have been of a type where the starter question can lead students into different, though connected, concepts of the mathematics curriculum. I now consider working the other way round: deciding upon a broader concept and considering how I might provide all students with access to a particular concept. I return to Pythagoras' Theorem as an example.

A problem-solving approach for teaching Pythagoras

In planning to teach Pythagoras we might ask ourselves questions such as:

✓ What is Pythagoras' Theorem essentially about?

✓ What other concepts are linked to Pythagoras' Theorem?

✓ What kinds of puzzle or problem might I pose to provide students with access to, and the opportunity to construct, an understanding of Pythagoras?

✓ What strategies might I use to cause students to practise and consolidate their understanding of Pythagoras' Theorem?

✓ What kind of development or enrichment ideas might I use to extend students' thinking?

The last three questions match planning criteria 1), 3) and 4) in the earlier list and, therefore, the planning framework is similar. The spider diagram below is an attempt to explore concepts that underpin and are linked to Pythagoras' Theorem. As it stands, there is much missing, such as taking a historical perspective to consider how the concept we know as Pythagoras' has roots in Egyptian, Babylonian, Chinese and Indian cultures. The issue of proving Pythagoras is another substantial area for consideration.

Having begun to explore the terrain, I need to decide what starting-point problem I might pose to help students construct an understanding of the theorem. My personal favourite is to

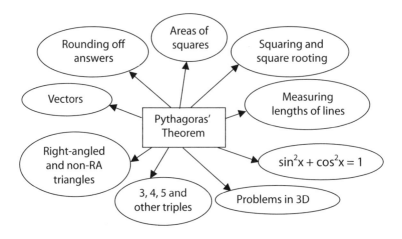

provide students with pegs and pegboards, so each person has ten or a dozen pegs of his or her chosen colour. The idea is to play a simple game called Four-in-a-square. Players take turns to place pegs in the board and the winner is the first person to place four pegs on the four corners of a square. Once a square has been made, students draw this on square grid paper and work out the following information from each square:

1 Write one side of the square using vector notation.
2 Calculate the area of the square.

As more 'slanted' squares emerge, the information can be collected together and fed back to the whole class, perhaps by making an 'instant' display using of lots of A4-size pieces of sugar paper, each with a vector and the area of the square written with a large marker pen. With 20 or so separate pieces of information around the room, students can engage with the task of trying to connect together the elements of a vector with the area of the square.

   Once students have begun to form an idea about what is happening they can draw other 'slanted' squares on square grid paper to check out whether the conjecture continues to hold. Although this is fundamentally what Pythagoras is all about, there is still much work for students to do. This is to 'see' the vector as the hypotenuse of a right-angled triangle and how the length of the vector can be calculated once the area of the square is known. Clearly, there is much emphasis here upon understanding key vocabulary, such as hypotenuse, right-angled triangle and square root.

More practise and consolidation

One strategy I find transferable to a multitude of situations and which is particularly useful when I want students to practise Pythagoras (and trigonometric calculations) works as follows. On 1cm² grid paper (and eventually on plain paper), students draw some right-angled triangles, initially with the two shorter sides having integer length. They then apply Pythagoras' Theorem to calculate the length of the hypotenuse. Having worked out this result to one decimal place, they measure (with a ruler) the length of the hypotenuse and check whether their calculated answer is the same as their measured result. Students do as many of these as they need to in order to consolidate their understanding of the procedure. (I develop issues of practise and consolidation in Chapter 13.) There is an issue here about trusting students and creating a situation where they can take the initiative and the responsibility to do as many calculations as they feel is necessary. In my experience, I find students who struggle with mathematics usually do many more examples than those who understand what the procedure is all about. This is one aspect of working with differentiated learning. Furthermore, and because I would teach Year 7 students how to program a graphical calculator, older students have the skill base to write a program for Pythagoras' procedure. Once such a program has been written, students feed information in and speedily get information back. Again, here there is the issue of differentiated outcomes and the importance of providing students with sufficiently challenging tasks, based upon having and using the basic tools for solving problems.

Extension tasks

Beyond working out the length of one of the short sides of a right-angled triangle, a further task is to explore what happens when squares are drawn on the sides of non right-angled triangles. This is intended to lead students to construct inequalities $a^2 + b^2 > c^2$ and $a^2 + b^2 < c^2$, depending upon whether the triangle has all acute angles or has one obtuse angle. Other problems and developments for students to work on are:

✓ Exploring what happens when semi-circles (or any similar shapes) are drawn on the sides of a right-angled triangle.
✓ Working out the distance between any two points (x_1, y_1) and (x_2, y_2).
✓ Finding out the length of the 3D diagonal in a cuboid.
✓ Finding different sets of Pythagorean triples.
✓ Connecting Pythagoras with the identity $\sin^2 x + \cos^2 x = 1$.
✓ Proving the result. There are very many proofs, yet the important issue is that students are encouraged to try and construct a proof themselves.

Using and applying Pythagoras' Theorem

The most difficult issue for students in using and applying any mathematical skill or concept is being able to recognise which tools they can use from their mathematical toolkit to help solve a problem. If students come to rely on their teacher to suggest which tool they might need to use, this creates a teacher-dependency where students are less likely to think for themselves. If, however, students are brought up in a problem-solving environment, where they are encouraged to become independent problem-solvers, they are better equipped to decide what mathematics they might bring to a less-obvious situation. The following problem, originally offered to me by Liz Meenan, opens up such a possibility and makes use of old packs of cards kindly donated by my local Bridge club.

1 Take a playing card. (I slice off a couple of mm from each long edge, thus creating dimensions of approximately 52mm by 90mm.)
2 Fold the top left-hand corner on to the bottom right-hand corner.
3 Fold the two 'triangular' bits over so you have something that is close enough to an equilateral triangle. These will become 'flaps' (see figure below).

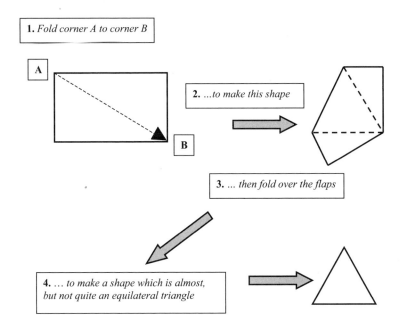

1. *Fold corner A to corner B*

A

B

2. *...to make this shape*

3. *... then fold over the flaps*

4. *... to make a shape which is almost, but not quite an equilateral triangle*

The problem is as follows:

> If the solid were a regular tetrahedron, what dimensions would any rectangular piece of card need to have?

Solving this problem requires students to:

✓ recognise the need to use Pythagoras' Theorem;
✓ manipulate surds;
✓ apply Pythagoras in a non-obvious context.

Once students have sorted this out, they can take a pair of scissors to the cards and snip away. I mention this to make the task accessible to students who might be too young to conceptualise Pythagoras but who can still have an opportunity to experience this tetrahedron-making process.

Even further developments

If we fold four such cards each time the same way these can be formed into an octahedron. This requires deft handiwork: having two pairs of hands may prove useful. Now, because a tetrahedron and an octahedron tessellate in 3D space, there is an opportunity to challenge the most confident of school-aged mathematicians to calculate the dihedral angles of the two solids and prove why they fill 3D space.

Alternatively, if we are interested in a visual impact, we can stick one tetrahedron on to each face of the octahedron and be amazed at the outcome – a compound of two (intersecting) tetrahedra. This process can be continued as more octahedra fit into the holes created by the last group of eight tetrahedra: then more tetrahedra will fit into the new set of holes.

What happens when more tetrahedra and octahedra are added is something I am still working on. I have an intuition about the eventual formation of a large octahedron at some point in this growth process … I have just not got there yet.

'Good' mathematical tasks that stand the test of time

The process I have gone through in this chapter – to consider what mathematics is, why and how I seek to teach mathematics and how I want students to experience mathematics – has implications for planning and determining the strategies and tasks I might use. Over recent years mathematics teaching has become evermore prescribed in terms of national strategies, levels and targets. This prescription has been backed by testing and inspection regimes. Mathematics teachers have been given greater guidance about how the prescribed curriculum 'should' be taught. As such, it has become increasingly difficult for teachers to prioritise time to create their constructions of what mathematics is and to decide for themselves how everything fits together, especially when they are presented with ready-made models and methods. Yet because there is no one way to teach mathematics, it is important to make such decisions for ourselves. Perhaps with the demise of the national strategies things will change for the better.

One thought has remained with me consistently throughout all the changes and curriculum iterations. If I have an interesting mathematical idea or a useful way of providing students with access to mathematics, this will hold true in my classroom whatever the curriculum looks like and whoever is directing proceedings. In order to be confident that the ideas we have are valuable and will stand the test of time, it is important to go in deep and ask the searching question: What is mathematics?

2

Strategies for teaching mathematics

In this chapter I consider the kinds of strategies at teachers' disposal for use in classrooms. Having a range of ways of teaching clearly supports students' different ways of learning. At this juncture I am conscious, however, of not wishing to jump on the preferred learning styles/visual, auditory, kinaesthetic (VAK) bandwagon. This is because I am troubled by the notion that individuals have a specific or a dominant learning style that can be empirically determined and am sceptical of comments I have heard, such as 'So and so is a kinaesthetic learner.' In reality, students respond to a variety of stimuli, so it is important to provide planned, eclectic approaches to teaching to create powerful learning opportunities. Furthermore, even if we could objectify preferred learning styles for different individuals, I am not sure what any teacher does with such information. For example, when I walk into a classroom I can take it for granted, with 100 per cent certainty, that there will be a range of students who have different levels of understanding and different approaches to learning with different amounts of food in their stomachs and who will be in different emotional states. Okay, so if I know this, what do I do with this information about levels and preferred learning styles for each of the 25 to 30 students present? How do I use such information to plan a lesson and how do I begin to teach it?

Recognising that different individuals learn at different rates and understand ideas to different depths merely indicates I need to employ, over time, a range of different teaching approaches and to use a range of different strategies, resources and stimuli to accommodate such differences. To provide a context to discuss different strategies I refer again to the seminal publication by the DES, *Mathematics from 5 to 16* (1985).

Mathematics as an essential element of communication

Mathematics might be considered a tool of communication in the following ways:

1 As a language containing its own specialised vocabulary.
2 As a shorthand requiring communicatees to understand signs and symbols.

As such, students need to learn the vocabulary, read the signs and understand the symbols. Specific mathematical vocabulary is clearly substantial. Trying to write as many mathematically related words beginning with the letter A as possible in two minutes is an interesting activity (I just came up with nine but missed three obvious ones). Perhaps you might want to try it. To make sense of vocabulary there needs to be hundreds of in-context opportunities where vocabulary is strategically and explicitly used. Here are four strategies I have used:

✓ Write mathematical words on the board that arise as a lesson progresses and ask students to copy these down. There could be a homework task here, to ask students to write a definition for each word or explain the list of words to someone at home.
✓ Construct mathematical dictionaries using loose-leaf A5 paper.
✓ Ask students to write the definition of a word with a picture to illustrate meaning and use for display purposes.
✓ Ask students to write about the work they are doing or have done.

This was a regular feature of GCSE coursework and although coursework no longer features at GCSE, students still need to develop the skills of how to write about mathematics from an early age. This is because when students can explain a mathematical process in writing, such as calculating the distance between two points or how to find the volume of a cylinder, they deepen their understanding. Although such concepts are in the domain of Key Stage 3 and Key Stage 4 students, this issue is even more important at primary level. So, for example, Key Stage 2 pupils might only do half as many multiplication calculations and then explain their understanding of what multiplication means. This would be time well spent. Learning how to communicate mathematical understanding and to become explicit about implicit knowledge is central to mathematical concept development.

Mathematics as a powerful tool

For students to appreciate mathematics as a powerful tool they need to be offered problems to work on so they can see how they use mathematics to reach solutions. There are basically two ways in which mathematics can be used; in pure and applied situations.

The first is about seeing mathematics as a set of systems, structures and relations underpinned by logical and abstract thinking where the ultimate power lies in constructing a proof. I frequently hear professional colleagues, usually at ATM conferences, refer to an 'elegant' proof. I have also seen undergraduates put their heads in their hands and exclaim in mock exasperation (I hope), 'Oh no, not the dreaded "P" word again!' The 'dreaded word' surfaced during a geometry module I had the pleasure to teach, during which I had the fun of repeatedly asking 'But can you prove it?'

Typical problems involving proof were:

✓ angle/circle theorems;
✓ proving why there are only five Platonic solids;
✓ folding a flat knot in a strip of paper, then proving the resulting shape is a regular pentagon;
✓ proving the centroid of a triangle is 1/3 of the distance between each vertex and the mid-point of the side opposite.

Regarding school mathematics, the challenge is to present problems so students can seek to create a proof of the solutions they produce. For example, proving:

✓ they have found all possible triangles on a nine-pin square geoboard;

✓ Pythagoras' Theorem;

✓ they have found all the tetrominoes;

✓ the addition of two odd numbers is even;

✓ the product of two odd numbers is odd;

✓ the sum of the internal angles of a triangle is 180°;

✓ the sum of consecutive triangular numbers is a square number.

A second challenge relates to 'real-life' problems. There are any number of these that require students to use or develop modelling skills. I am conscious, however, of the dangers of creating pseudo contexts that provide an 'excuse' for doing mathematics, such as the builder who uses formulae to determine how many different coloured paving flags are needed to build a patio. I develop this issue in greater depth in Chapter 8. Real, real-life contexts impact directly on young children's and adolescents' lives. For example, attention to healthy eating opens up marvellous opportunities for students to engage in the mathematics of food and energy. Through mathematics students can make sense of the calories we need to provide us with our energy requirement, the kind of exercise that burns up calories and the fat content of different foods. Exploring average daily calorific input on the one hand and exercise on the other and looking at ways of producing mathematical models to explain these can also open up cross-curricular opportunities. Similarly, exploring issues of smoking, perhaps carrying out a 'truth' survey and using data collected from the whole school, will provide enormous opportunities for students to work on the mathematics of health-related issues. I have written about this idea, as a cross-curricular theme, in *Creating Positive Classrooms* (2004).

Appreciation of relationships within mathematics

Mathematics is fundamentally about appreciating and understanding relationships, for example between:

✓ the lengths of the sides in a right-angled triangle;
✓ angles through circle theorems;
✓ the Fibonacci Sequence and the Golden Ratio;
✓ height and circumference of head;
✓ coordinates and vectors;
✓ a quadratic function and the turning point of its graph.

Creating opportunities for students to see relationships and form connections between mathematical concepts is important to deepen confidence and competence within the subject.

Awareness of the fascination of mathematics and imagination, initiative and flexibility of mind in mathematics

I have put these two together because they seem to be closely connected. For students to be fascinated by mathematics places a substantial responsibility upon teachers to provide potentially fascinating ideas for students to explore.

*Mathematics is not only taught because it is useful. It should also be a source of delight and wonder, offering pupils intellectual excitement and an appreciation of its essential creativity. (*Non-Statutory Guidance *[1989, para 2.5 p. A3])*

The quote fits perfectly with this aim; seeking to achieve it is what makes teaching mathematics such an interesting and intriguing challenge. I cannot emphasise enough the value of puzzlement as a strategy to fascinate students, to cause them to use their imagination and be prepared to work in flexible ways. An example is: using brightly coloured pieces of A4 paper, ask them to make two folds in their paper that intersect and so neither fold is parallel to the edges of the paper. The problem is to measure one of the angles at the intersection between the two fold lines and one of the angles where a line meets the edge and use this information to calculate all the other angles.

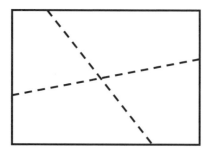

An extension task is to label one angle (at the intersection point) *a* and one angle (at the edge) *b* and then to write the size of every other angle in terms of *a* and *b*.

The task can be developed in different ways to challenge students. One is to fold/draw a line perpendicular to one of the two initial lines so a triangle is created in the middle of the sheet. At issue is students recognizing how angles can be determined from a minimum amount of information ... and not a textbook in sight!

Here is an anecdote about a lesson I had the privilege to observe in January 2005. The purpose of the lesson was to revise for a test.

Revision class

The students are revising for a science test they will be doing the following week. The teacher has asked a boy to come to the front of the classroom with his exercise book and use this to make up and ask questions about the work the students have done. The boy quietly asks a number of questions and as each question is read out members of the class eagerly wave their hands in the air, each wanting to be the one to answer the question. The boy points to one of his classmates, an answer is received and he moves on to ask his next question.

Next, a diminutive girl comes to the front. I can barely see her face, partly because she is so small and partly because her exercise book, which she proudly holds, is partially covering her face. Her voice, however, booms out as she asks her questions. As before, the other children strive to be chosen – some are almost out of their desks in their enthusiasm to provide answers. The little girl seems as if she is imbued with assertiveness as she carefully chooses who is to answer each question, pointing to her classmates in a determined, careful manner. The teacher, meanwhile, appears on the surface not to be doing anything.

This is a shining illustration of a teacher being able to 'take a back seat' because she has already done all the hard work of teaching by:

✓ instilling a sense of responsibility in her children;
✓ utilising a teaching strategy where students are temporarily invited to play the role of (another) teacher;
✓ creating a positive relationship with the class;
✓ demonstrating that learning is not just 'fun': it is significantly important.

The above anecdote occurred on a bright sunny morning in January 2005 in a class of seven- and eight-year-old children. The school is situated on the outskirts of Asmara, Eritrea. There were 42 children in the class. I know this because there were 21 small bench-type desks in the room and a colleague reliably informed me there were three children to each bench two years prior. The only visible resource was a blackboard with a scratched surface and some sticks of white chalk.

Furthermore, as the lesson was conducted in Tigrinya, I could not understand a word of what the children were saying, though it was not too difficult to see enthusiastic and motivated children actively engaged in and taking responsibility for their learning with a seemingly relaxed and skilled teacher at work.

In the following four chapters about surprises, people-math, using practical equipment and approaches to mental mathematics, I offer further examples of the kinds of strategies at any teacher's disposal. However, before moving on to Chapter 3, I have a concern relating to the strategy of writing one's objectives, which I discuss below.

The orthodoxy of objectives

Many years ago I saw a cartoon in a newspaper of a person dressed in medieval clothes sitting on a rock in the pose of 'The Thinker'. A thought bubble read: 'I think ... therefore I am a subversive.' The notion of teachers writing lesson objectives on the board has, over the past few years, become a received orthodoxy. In some schools I hear of senior staff and heads of department spending valuable time checking that classroom teachers are compliant in carrying out this new orthodoxy. Such checking is also on the agendas of Ofsted and local authority inspectors/ advisors. Children, it seems, are no longer to be 'left in the dark' about their teacher's intentions. Transparency rules, and learning follows directly from teaching just as night follows day ... If only life in classrooms was quite so simple!

I believe it is vitally important for teachers to discuss with a class all kinds of issues relating to learning, such as:

✓ the approaches a teacher believes are important to support students' learning;
✓ helping students understand the value of what they are learning;
✓ the value of students engaging in learning in positive, responsible ways.

Whether I choose to share with a class what I intend 'us' to work on is a professional decision I choose to make. I do not want other people who occasionally pop into my classroom and therefore cannot begin to understand the nature of the relationships I have with a class to determine my teaching behaviours for me. In order to deconstruct the value of writing specific, narrow learning objectives I raise four concerns and discuss each of these below. They are:

1 Teacher autonomy and professional judgement;
2 Differentiated learning and continuation lessons;
3 Student responsibility;
4 Surprises and unpredictability, ambiguity and uncertainty.

Teacher autonomy and professional judgement

For any teacher to learn about teaching, we need to engage with issues of autonomy and autocracy. If all I ever did as a teacher was what some higher and supposedly wiser authority had told me to do, and this person had passed on prescribed methods and ways of working, then my teaching capability would have been severely limited. However, I was fortunate enough to have a first head of department, in my formative years of teaching, who encouraged autonomous and creative thinking.

Of course, there was a basic framework (scheme of work) and support mechanisms (including personal and curriculum development opportunities) in place, and I relied upon these to help me with my development. These provided a 'safety net', which was important to help me come to know myself as a teacher, to extend my teaching approaches and decide when to play safe. I was encouraged to try out a range of strategies, to take risks and to share what I was doing within the department, and this created a culture of openness and trust.

My first concern, therefore, about writing objectives on the board is of teachers doing so because they have been told to do so. This undermines autonomy and subverts professional judgement. Of course, if a teacher chooses to write objectives on the board because he or she firmly believes this is an important part of the learning process, because he or she has analysed and rationalised the reasons for doing so, this is another matter altogether. This is an example of a teacher making an autonomous professional judgement and this must be respected. However, the prescriptive nature of governmental education initiatives over the last few years means some newly qualified teachers have primarily been trained to teach a three-part lesson format and to share objectives and desired learning outcomes. The result is that some of the recent generations of teachers are far more comfortable with the format of three- (or four-) part lessons, sharing objectives, etc. than more experienced colleagues, who feel their methods no longer conform to the 'required' model. From a student perspective – five lessons a day, five days a week – many come to expect to be told what they are going to learn to do during the next lesson of whatever subject they are studying: they will soon be suffering from repetitive objective syndrome!

Differentiated learning and continuation lessons

Learning takes place at different speeds and to different depths of cognition for different people. As such, if I, as a teacher, manipulate the learning (or the outcomes of learning) so all students achieve the same objective in a lesson, I must have moved the lesson along at too fast a pace for some and at too slow a pace for others. Teaching to a 'one-size-fits-all' pace will not benefit a class because there are as many paces and depths of learning in a class as there are students present. For example, if I pose a problem such as 'finding all the different nets of a cube', students will inevitably find solutions by working at different paces and in different ways. I see little value in moving a whole class towards an answer that there are a given amount of different nets if, by doing so, my intervention becomes an interference. I do not want to run the risk of mathematically interfering with those students who are trying to find out this information for themselves, at a pace commensurate with their current level of cognition. Of course, I have a responsibility to deepen the mathematical experience of those students who quickly find all the solutions, and to do this I need to have other extension tasks, such as 'try to prove you have all the nets'. Taking students' differentiated learning (both speed and depth) into account meant many of the lessons I taught in secondary classrooms were continuation lessons. A new topic would be introduced in one lesson and continued over the following five, six or even ten lessons. How far different students developed their understanding of the central concepts within the topic varied considerably. Sustaining a topic over a period of two, three or four weeks meant students had opportunities to develop their thinking, explore ideas to different depths and learn one of the most important life skills of taking personal responsibility for their work. I develop this below. However, had I begun each lesson by writing an objective on the board, this would have fragmented students' experiences of mathematics and reduced their learning to 'bite-size' pieces.

Fragmenting mathematics is something we can leave to many of the textbooks on the market: we don't have to subscribe to this style of teaching in order to fulfil a potentially ill-thought-out approach to learning mathematics.

Student responsibility

The phrase 'students taking responsibility for their learning' rolls easily off the tongue, yet is a highly complex issue. For students to recognise the importance of taking responsibility requires them to inhabit a classroom culture that encourages autonomy and celebrates individualism. There is an important parallel here with teachers being similarly valued for their professional autonomy. When students make autonomous, mathematical decisions they ultimately become more responsible learners. If I am to educate my students to take responsibility, then I must also learn when to take a step back, to loosen my authority and to trust, over time, that students will 'do the business'. All this is connected to classroom culture, to my expectations of myself as a teacher and to students as learners.

A key aspect of responsibility is connected to students setting their own goals within a supportive, negotiated framework. Personal goal-setting is something that must arise naturally as a consequence of students developing and exploring ideas. If student responsibility is to be taken seriously it is not feasible for the teacher to take the responsibility of setting a single objective because individuals in a class will inevitably have different goals to achieve particularly if a topic continues over a sequence of lessons.

Surprises and unpredictability, ambiguity and uncertainty

Finally, I am at a loss to understand how objective-setting can embrace surprises or countenance unpredictability. Deep learning occurs when students make sense of something they have had to puzzle out, something they have had to work hard on. Some students may have had cause to backtrack, to be systematic, to look for blips in a set of data or try to make sense of unexpected outcomes. Mathematics holds very many surprises, and here is one such example.

> On the circumference of a circle draw two nodes and join them together with an arc. This arc splits the circle up into two regions. Now draw a circle with three nodes and join them with three arcs and we have a diagram with four regions. With four nodes we have six arcs and eight regions and with five nodes, ten arcs and sixteen regions. With 6 nodes we do get 15 arcs but do not get 32 regions! (This assumes that no three arcs meet at a single point.) So, while the number of arcs conforms to the triangular number sequence (1, 3, 6, 10, 15 ...), the number of nodes does not conform to powers of two. A situation that appeared as though the sequence 2, 4, 8, 16, 32 ... was emerging produces something quite different.

The following chapter contains further surprises.

Mathematics is more than a list of content knowledge (Pythagoras, trigonometry, etc.) to be learnt in bite-size pieces. It is a beautiful, intriguing and mind-blowing subject that can encourage learners to engage in deep, independent and shared thought. Through mathematics students can learn to make choices, take responsibility and to develop their understanding at different paces and to different depths. Objective-setting when framed in a narrow sense of 'this is what you are going to learn' militates against ambiguity and uncertainty, important aspects of mathematics that students need to understand. On the other hand, students need to recognise there is an abundance of situations in mathematics where proof rules okay and where generality lies at its heart.

PART 2

3

Mathematical surprises

Surprises – well, pleasant ones – can sometimes be magical, sometimes interesting, but are always worth experiencing. Things that surprise me make me to stop in my tracks, take a second and third look, causing me to analyse events to try to make sense of the phenomenon that has captured my attention. My analysis might be to extol the beauty of something, to proclaim an interest or to want to capture a memory of it and possibly share it with others. Walking one early morning in Scotland on New Year's Day 2002 produced several surprises. The first was to be setting out on the hills before 8.00 a.m., when many respectable folk would have been nursing a hangover. The second was to see snow-cast mountains to the west take on a pink hue, and a pale then piercingly bright-yellow sun cover the landscape to the east. The third surprise was to attain the summit cairn by 10.00 a.m.

But wait a moment – I am meant to be writing a book about teaching mathematics, so what is all this blathering about winter hill walking? The strong connection for me lies in seeing teaching mathematics as an extension of many things I do in life beyond the classroom. Walking the hills is about freedom, challenge, exploration, making decisions, using navigational skills, making and recovering from errors, being exhilarated, enjoying the simple things in life and opening myself up to surprises. Mathematics is similarly rich in surprises, in 'Aha!' moments, in challenges and struggles, as well as providing many opportunities to grab students' attention.

Grabbing students' attention

Whilst it would be absurd to suggest every lesson needs to be some kind of performance, there are times when I want to have fun, to engage students with challenging problems. To try to achieve this and to grab students' attention I work on the mystery, intrigue and the surprise of mathematics both through the starting points I use and the way I offer them. There is always the danger, however, that 'good' starting points may be seen merely as pleasant, entertaining, attention-grabbing devices intended to sustain students' interest over a short period of time. Yet effective learning environments are about much more than the teacher providing starter tasks. What happens over subsequent lessons, when students are expected to develop a task or practise and consolidate knowledge, is crucial to helping them grapple with and make sense of mathematics.

Students also need to expect to have to work hard on a skill, to practise and get better at it. This is no different from the pianist practising his scales or the athlete building up her fitness: both require hard work and dedication. The magic elixir I look for is how to create classroom environments where students are prepared to work over 'dead' times. This is so they see for themselves that practise, in order to get better at mathematics and to experience the pleasure that lies within the surprising world of mathematics, is worth doing.

There are many problems that provide surprises. Below are some of my favourites.

IRATical surprises

IRAT is my acronym for an Isosceles Right-Angled Triangle. The problem involves an exploration of what happens when IRATs are folded 0, 1, 2, 3 and 4 times and each time cut down the line of symmetry. I usually begin this problem by holding up an IRAT and asking everyone to write down some things they know about the shape, followed by asking individuals (though not using a 'hands-up' approach) to say what they have written down.

Quite quickly, a list of the properties of the shape emerges. This list almost always includes its colour and the fact it is a piece of paper! All comments offered are gratefully accepted and written on the board.

After a short time enough information is usually provided to describe the shape accurately, establish its name and become explicit about its properties. Next, I take a pair of scissors to the shape and cut it along the line of symmetry to produce two similar IRATs, each one being half the area of the original. The diagram below illustrates this, with the dotted line being the line of symmetry along which the original triangle is cut.

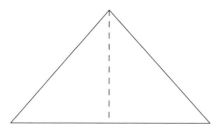

The problem develops as follows:

1   Fold a new IRAT in half down the line of symmetry. A triangle half the size of the original will be formed, which will have its own line of symmetry. Now cut through this new line of symmetry and see what happens. Before revealing the result students could be asked to visualise and describe what shapes are formed in terms of name and area. It might be appropriate to use this to discuss ideas of similarity and congruence. This provides an in-context opportunity to engage with vocabulary.

2   With two folds and a cut, a square of area 1/2 and two smaller IRATs of area 1/4 are formed. At this juncture the students could be asked to find all the different shapes, and prove they have found them all, by joining the three pieces together by same length edge.

3   Now, start again with a new IRAT and make two folds, each one along the line of symmetry. Cut the shape in half and see what happens.

4   The surprising result is as follows:

After 0 folds and a cut, 2 shapes are formed.
After 1 fold and a cut, 3 shapes are formed.
After 2 folds and a cut, 4 shapes are formed.
After 3 folds and a cut ...

Several possibilities open up:

✓ Visualisation and discussion
✓ Use of vocabulary: conservation of area, perimeter, and surds.
✓ Working with simple fractions.
✓ Adding fractions to check all the pieces from each experiment total 1.
✓ Equivalent fractions.
✓ Predicting the number and the sizes of pieces so formed.
✓ Writing the sizes of the pieces formed as decimal values or as percentages of the whole.

Because the 'sequence' of the number of shapes develops 2, 3, 4, 6, 9 ... there is much for students to explore and sort out. All the time, possibilities exist for exploring fractions with denominators of powers of 2. Trying to predict how the sequence develops is a sizeable challenge and will certainly be a challenge for Key Stage 4 students. The next idea is intended to help students develop concepts of negative powers of 2 acting as the denominator of fractions.

An opportunity to grapple with the meaning of $1/2^{-1}$

The denominators gained from the smallest triangle formed as each IRAT is successively folded and cut are halves, quarters, eighths, etc. After three folds we have sixteenths or ($\frac{1}{2} \times \frac{1}{2} \times \frac{1}{2} \times \frac{1}{2}$), which can be written as $1/2^4$. By working this sequence of sizes of triangles backwards from $1/2^4$ to the original IRAT, we gain the following information:

Smallest fraction		Index form
1/16	=	2^{-4} or $1/2^4$
1/8	=	2^{-3} or $1/2^3$
1/4	=	2^{-2} or $1/2^2$
1/2	=	2^{-1} or $1/2^1$

Continuing this pattern, the following results can be gained:

1/1	=	2^0 or $1/2^0$

This is the original IRAT of area 1. The next result is:

1/½	=	2^1 or $1/2^{-1}$

This must be two of the original IRATs added together, which, therefore, has an area of 2. Although this does not prove that $1/2^{-1}$ is equal to 2, it does provide a robust visual aid to help demonstrate it. What I particularly like about this demonstration is being able to see a piece of paper that has an area of $1/2^{-1}$. Being able to demonstrate any abstract concept in some kind of concrete way is useful. Looking for opportunities to help students make sense of underlying mathematical principles is also one of the great joys and challenges of teaching mathematics.

Conservation of area and working with surds

The richness of any problem is measured by the variety of mathematical concepts up for grabs. Before leaving the IRAT problem, therefore, I offer a challenge for students who have knowledge of surds. The task involves calculating the perimeter of shapes re-formed from the pieces produced after folding and cutting IRATs.

Given the original triangle has edge lengths 2, $\sqrt{2}$ and $\sqrt{2}$ (in order to have an area of 1), the perimeter of the parallelogram formed by these two half-size triangles is $P = 2 + 2\sqrt{2}$. The perimeter of the square, formed by joining the resulting pieces from no folds and one cut, is $P = 4$.

The problem develops by making all possible shapes created from the three pieces formed from one fold and one cut and joined by equal length of edge. These are:

- ✓ one parallelogram;
- ✓ one isosceles trapezium;
- ✓ one rectangle;
- ✓ one asymmetrical pentagon;
- ✓ one symmetrical hexagon;
- ✓ two asymmetrical hexagons.

As before, the perimeter of each shape can be calculated: for example, the perimeter of the parallelogram below is also $P = 2 + 2\sqrt{2}$.

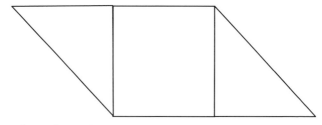

I can also ask students to prove they have found all possible shapes. The IRAT problem is therefore packed with rich potential and can be used in various ways to support learning.

A rich source of surprise resides within 3D mathematics, and this is the focus of the next section.

A 3D surprise

One idea is based upon making square-based pyramids to demonstrate the volume of the pyramid is one third of the volume of the cube into which it fits. The problem can be given in different ways according to students' existing knowledge. The first version would be appropriate for students who have previously worked with Pythagoras' Theorem and in 3D mathematics, such as drawing nets and making solids. Under such circumstances, I offer the following problem statement:

Make a square-based pyramid with side length and perpendicular height 15cm and with the apex perpendicular to one corner of the base.

Depending upon age and mathematical experience, other versions I might offer students are:

1 The dimensions of the pyramid but not a picture of the net.
2 A scale drawing of the net to reproduce on sugar paper.
3 The shapes of the faces as templates and ask them to design a net.
4 The completed net to cut out and assemble.

How simple or complex a teacher decides to make this problem will depend upon all kinds of circumstances and classroom contexts. Mathematically, the fourth of these tasks may seem to lack challenge. However, the task is something I want all students to experience within a scheme of work and I must take into consideration students who have wide-ranging aptitudes. When the pyramids have been made, I usually borrow three models and double-hinge pairs of edges together using tape. All three pyramids form a cube and though this does not prove the formula for the volume of a pyramid it is a useful demonstration to help explain why the 1/3 appears in the formula.

Another 3D surprise

This idea is similar to the previous one, although possibly more surprising, and certainly provides an amazing result. The problem statement I work with is:

Make a square-based pyramid so the apex is perpendicular to the centre of the base with side length X and a perpendicular height of ½x.

Ideally, I want students to make a lot of these, although once they have worked out the required dimensions for one solid they can use this as a template to make others more speedily. By joining six of these together in the shape of the net of a cube (of which there are eleven different possibilities) a most interesting outcome occurs. This is that the six pyramids fold up into a cube. However, the surprise of this particular problem is yet to unfold … literally. By unfolding the six pyramids and wrapping the six square faces around another congruent cube, a rhombic dodecahedron is produced. Even more amazing is that the rhombic dodecahedron tessellates 3D space. This could lead to an exploration of other solids that tessellate 3D space.

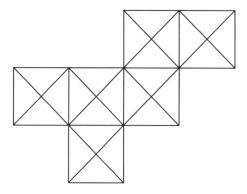

I have also used the construction of the net as a context for students to practise trigonometric calculations by calculating the angles of the triangular faces for each net. A more complex problem is to try to calculate the dihedral or the 'solid' angles of each pyramid. This problem will provide the strongest mathematicians with something of a challenge.

Other potential surprises

Writing a three-digit number, reversing the digits, finding the difference, reversing this answer and adding it to the result from the earlier subtraction to produce the result 1089 has the potential to create surprise. This surprise might be enhanced if the teacher happens to have 1089 stuck on his or her back and at some point 'carelessly' turns around to reveal the 'answer' to the class. Put a banana in a filing cabinet prior to a class entering the room and hold a conversation about the probability of different events happening. At some point, ask what the probability is of finding a banana in the filing cabinet. It may cause a surprise ... and some amusement.

Of course, surprises and any teacher's inclination to incorporate them into lessons, the way a teacher presents mathematical ideas and the fun he or she seeks to have is all part of the culture of the classroom. What is important to this teacher is to look for opportunities to have fun, to create surprises and to actively demonstrate that enjoyment is a key feature of learning. There exist many other surprises to present to students, but if beauty is in the eye of the beholder then surprises are in the eyes of the surprised. Of course, we can never guarantee anything, especially in classrooms. However, we can choose to work on creating opportunities for surprises to occur and, therefore, provide students with mathematical experiences from which they can gain pleasure and engage in the puzzlement and the power of mathematics ... the three Ps.

Intrigue and mystery

I remember a former colleague who often used intrigue as a powerful way to gain students' attention. He suggested that taking a cardboard box into a lesson and pulling out the most mundane objects creates a sense of intrigue and stimulates students' natural instincts to want to know. I have had enormous fun at times using the same strategy and it always seems to work ... It's a mystery.

A situation I frequently used with groups to create a sense of intrigue and fun occurred when I set up the 'Painted Cube' problem, a well-known problem described in many publications. As a class enters the room I surreptitiously say to one student: 'The answer to the question I'll ask you is "It's a bucket."' To the next student I would say: 'The answer to the question I'll ask you is "It's quick-drying paint."' To the third student: "The answer to the question I'll ask you is "It's red."'

When the class are all assembled I hold up the cardboard box and ask the first student: 'What is this?' To the second I ask: 'What is in this bucket?' and to the third: 'What is the colour of the paint in this bucket?' After each correct answer has been provided I produce a white $3 \times 3 \times 3$ cube made from 27 linking cubes. I drop it into the cardboard box and pull out a red 3x3x3 cube. Corny I know, but this always seems to captivate students and acts as a useful precursor to the problem to be worked on. What never fails to amuse me and, I guarantee, always happens, is some time later in the lesson when I casually leave the cardboard box on the side some student looks inside and says something such as 'I knew there was another cube in the box!'

What I have described is about using intrigue as a strategy, as an element of a teaching style, to focus students' attention on a task. Mathematics, of course, holds many of its own mysteries and can provide students with much to think about. Some mysteries might be:

✓ Why the angle bisectors of a triangle meet at a common point.
✓ Why the side bisectors of a triangle meet at another, different point to the angle bisectors (unless the triangle is equilateral).
✓ Why, when successive terms of the Fibonacci Sequence are divided into one another, the answer settles out to 1.618 ... or 0.618 (depending upon which way round the division calculations are carried out).
✓ Why a tetrahedron and an octahedron tessellate in 3D space.
✓ Why folding a strip of paper into a flat knot produces a regular pentagon.
✓ Why the circumference of a circle is always three-and-a-bit times the length of the diameter.
✓ Why ...

Finally, of my favourite mysteries is based upon the following problem.

✓ Take a strip of paper and label the ends A and B.
✓ Make a fold line fairly close to end A.
✓ On this fold line write the number 1.
✓ Now I ask students to enter into a pretence that the distance from end A to the fold line marked 1 is 1/3 of the length of the whole strip.

The argument develops as follows.

If this length is 1/3 of the whole, the remaining length from fold 1 to end B is 2/3 of the whole strip, and if I fold the distance between 1 and B in half I must create a length 1/3 of the whole strip.

A   1   2   B

On this fold write the number 2

The distance from 2 to B is now a better approximation to 1/3 than the distance from 1 to A. By folding the distance between A and 2 in half, to gain fold 3, we gain an even better approximation to 1/3. By continuing this folding sequence to gain a few more folds something interesting happens. The seventh fold

A   1   3 5(7)   2   4 6(8)   B

is virtually the same as the fifth fold and the eighth fold will coincide (visually) with fold number six.

The mathematical explanation is that an iterative function, based upon the bisection method, occurs: as the number of folds increases the approximation to 1/3 gets closer. While this will not be a mystery to anyone who has worked on the problem, it can certainly appear mysterious to those who have not. Using a similar method to produce a fifth, a seventh and any fraction with a prime denominator is a worthy challenge, particularly as the solution is so beautifully logical.

Teacher, performer, actor or just being oneself

At the beginning of this chapter I mentioned the dangers of students coming to expect some kind of performance from their teacher. If students' contributions to lessons are largely dependent upon their teacher's performance, the downside is all too obvious.

Teachers engage in varying degrees in the art of performance and some will act in ways intended to create fun and laughter. However, learning mathematics also requires students to engage with difficulties, sometimes to enter uncomfortable zones and to be prepared to work with complexity; at other times students need to work hard at practising a skill. If students are ultimately to take responsibility for their learning, they need to recognise their teachers as honest, open people with strengths and frailties, excitements and disappointments. Students need to recognise that their teachers work hard to support their learning, but cannot do the learning for them.

Similarly, neither can one teacher's style be translated into another's. We can share ideas that work for ourselves in our classrooms. We can suggest the use of strategies and resources that have enabled students to engage purposefully in lessons. We can help one another with the lessons we plan, but at the end of the day we have to take ownership of our lessons and how we teach them. Ownership, in turn, arises from the risks a teacher is able or prepared to take, perhaps when trying something out for the first time. Ownership depends upon the depth to which we reflect upon our teaching and how interested we were about what occurred in a lesson; whether there were specific moments that made us feel contented or dissatisfied.

4

People-math

There are very many tasks that fall under the title of 'people-math'. Below are some ideas Peter and I have used, almost always with great success and much fun. Many more can be found in Alan Bloomfield and Bob Vertes' books *People Maths: Hidden Depths* and *More People, More Maths* via the ATM (www.atm.org.uk).

Such problems involve students getting out of their seats, leaving their desks and carrying out tasks in active, communal ways. This might appear to be a high-risk strategy, particularly if students are not used to working in such ways: as such, the ideas in this chapter need to be read with a sanity/health warning and treated with care. Setting up people-math tasks depends upon several factors. These include:

✓ The value a teacher ascribes to active lessons and active learning.
✓ The relationship a teacher has with a class.
✓ Reasons, from a mathematical perspective, to use such tasks.
✓ Reasons, from a generic learning perspective, to use such tasks.
✓ The size of the room.
✓ The teacher's energy levels.
✓ Whether any support exists, e.g. a learning support teacher, a colleague or a trainee teacher.
✓ Whether the lesson is being observed.

With regard to the first point, the values we take with us into the classroom have a massive impact upon how we teach, the resources and strategies we choose to use and the ways we respond to those we teach. In considering the second, I argue that using such people-math tasks can enhance teacher–student relationships. Of course, the converse can also be argued: however, I do not see the use of people-math ideas as a whether or not argument; I see it as a discussion about why and a decision about when. I develop issues pertaining to the third point in the remainder of this chapter. Finding ways of tapping into different modes of teaching is the issue raised by point four. This is important if we acknowledge the different ways learning happens. Using different approaches in the classroom to vary how students experience mathematics is central to the issue of tapping into their different intelligences. Much has been written about this, particularly through the work of Howard Gardner on multiple intelligences (see Moon and Shelton-Mayes, 1994).

Room size is clearly something to consider if the usual room is too small, or if there are fixtures such as benches this may create difficulties. However, one thing teachers are good at is making things happen and overcoming obstacles. If working on a people-math activity is seen as important, one might swap rooms with a colleague, utilise the school hall or go outside. With the sixth point in mind, we cannot of course legislate for how we might feel. Neither can we predict the way a class appears when they enter the room. We can only adapt ourselves to circumstances: again, this is something teachers build up high levels of skills in. With regard to the seventh, utilising the presence of another adult can have many benefits, particularly when working in highly active ways. Finally, when considering the last point, I strongly advocate the use of any people-math tasks whether in the presence of an inspector or another person who is observing a lesson. I speak from many first-hand experiences of being observed. If you are feeling really brave, or perhaps a little subversive, you might invite the inspector/observer to participate. Active involvement is, after all, is the best way to learn.

The first activity is one Peter often uses and calls 'Hands and feet'.

Hands and feet

Feet are worth 5 when they touch the floor, hands are worth 1 when they touch the floor otherwise they are worth 0. I invite five students to the front of the class and as a group ask them to make a total of 33. This can be made up in two ways, i.e. 5 feet and 8 hands or 6 feet and 3 hands. The group now has to organise itself so that just 6 feet and 3 hands are in contact with the floor. There often very quickly emerges a leader within the group who tells the others to 'stand on one leg' or 'put both hands down' in order to achieve their target. The smaller the number, the harder it is to make as several students have to score zero, so aren't allowed to put hands or feet on the floor. I don't allow them to use furniture, so they give each other piggy-backs, balance on their knees or lay flat on their tummies with knees bent and arms out looking like they are sky-diving. Clearly I am heading towards some basic algebra, with a simultaneous equation not far away, i.e. 5f + 8h = 33 and 6f + 3h = 33.

This may sound like a risky activity in terms of behaviour management. Peter obviously decides when to use this puzzle both in terms of the mathematics he wants pupils to work on and the appropriateness of the activity with regard to the class he is working with. Mathematically, for any given amount of quadrupeds (q), the minimum is a zero and the maximum is $12q$. As with any activity, students need to be aware of what mathematics they have been engaging with – this is about where such an activity leads.

Sitting in a ring of chairs and giving everyone a number

One furniture arrangement is to place chairs in a ring and desks around the edge of the room. This means once the activity has come to an end, students can turn their chairs around and work at the desks. Thus for the remainder of the lesson students face the wall: a different if not interesting arrangement. Prioritising the time required to rearrange furniture relates to the impor-tance anyone places upon people-math activities. This relates to pedagogy; to exploiting different ways of supporting students' learning … everything is connected.

An interesting phenomenon I have observed on many occasions when using this task relates to the reluctance of some students to sit next to someone of the opposite sex! Often, when students see the furniture in a ring, they arrange themselves in an arc of boys, a space, an arc of girls and another space. Before long, however, and as an outcome of the task, students lose their inhibitions about who they find themselves sitting next to. Everybody needs to be given a number on a piece of card from 1 up to n where n is the number of people in the circle.

Swapping places

This is probably the task that I have had more fun and laughter from than any other, whether working with seven year olds or adults. I call out instructions such as 'Swap places if you are …'

- ✓ 'a multiple of three.'
- ✓ 'one less than a multiple of two.'
- ✓ 'a number greater than 5 and less than 12.'
- ✓ 'a divisor of 36.'
- ✓ 'a prime number.'
- ✓ 'a square number.'
- ✓ 'a Fibonacci number.'
- ✓ 'two less than a multiple of five.'

There are, of course, many other instructions to cause students to swap places. Placing sequences of numbers on large strips of sugar paper around the walls may be a useful resource to help students remember and familiarise themselves with the sequences.

At some point, having given a rule, I remove my chair and take another person's place. This means someone else will not have a chair to sit on. Something that always occurs, on the dozens of occasions in a wide variety of contexts, is a slow-dawning realisation that somebody doesn't have a chair to sit on.

Momentarily, the focus of attention is on this person to stand in the space and call out a rule. At this point the game takes on a much greater urgency! Before long people are dashing across the ring determined not to be the person without a chair. Despite the numerous occasions I have played this game, and the way some students, including adults, have hurled themselves across the ring, nobody has ever managed to injure his or herself. However, I recognise there exists degrees of risk and, therefore, I always check there are no sharp edges or desk corners outside the ring or bags or coats inside the ring that could cause a possible injury. One occasion demanded some creativity in order to include one student who (already) had a broken leg.

Some continuation tasks are for students to:

✓ write down as many of the different sequences as they can remember, perhaps discussing them in pairs or in a small group first of all;
✓ write out some of the sequences and extend them, or perhaps try to take some sequences backwards;
✓ make connections between multiples and displacements. For example, the numbers 2, 5, 8, 11, 14 are each a displacement of 1 from multiples of 3, or $3n - 1$ (for $n = 1, 2, 3 ...$).

A more complex task is an idea I call the 'Intersecting sequences' problem, more frequently known as the 'Chinese remainder problem'.

Intersecting sequences problem

This problem again uses numbers in a ring where I ask students to move according to the rule: 'Find the person, and stay with the person, who is two more than your number.' Obviously, the highest odd- and the highest even-numbered people will not have anyone to find, but these two people will be found by two members of the class. The effect will be to separate the class into two groups: the even $(2n)$ numbers and the odd $(2n - 1)$ numbers (again for $n = 1, 2, 3 ...$). Asking the two people with the highest numbers to stay seated next to each other can be a useful strategy. Two resulting groups, the odds and the evens, will then be able to sit down in sequential order. I ask each person to write one of these sequence labels ($2n$ or $2n - 1$) on the back of his or her numbered card.

The next task is similar: 'Find the person who is three more than your number.' This produces the sequences $3n$, $3n - 1$ and $3n - 2$. Again, I work on students' understanding of the idea of sequences, and once the three groups have formed I ask students to call out their numbers in order. Sometimes, for a bit more fun, I ask them to call out their numbers as quickly as possible, or as noisily as possible, or in a voice that indicates their love and passion for their number. This may appear just a bit of 'daftness' on my part. It is.

Mathematically, the important concept is for students to see how the sequences 2, 5, 8, 11, 14 ... and 1, 4, 7, 10, 13 ... are related to multiples of 3. Under this task they are either in the $3n$, the $3n - 1$ or the $3n - 2$ sequence. Again, students write one of these sequence labels on the back of their card, so at this point everyone has two labels written on the back of their numbered card.

Now comes the crunch problem, and this is set up by asking students to form groups with people who have both the same labels written on the back of their cards. Thus, students with both $2n$ and $3n$ will form the sequence 6, 12, 18, 24 ... or $6n$. Those with both $2n$ and $3n$-1 form the sequence 2, 8, 14, 20, 26 ... or $6n - 4$. At this point different challenges can ensue, such as trying to find labels for other pairs of intersecting sequences. For example, which numbers are in both $3n - 2$ and $4n - 1$ sequences? The ultimate problem is to try to find a way of predicting what the intersecting label is for any pair of sequences. This will challenge most students – and some inspectors.

Every other person sits down problem

Again, starting with everyone in a ring, this task begins with everybody standing up in order from 1 to n. Number 1 sits down, then 3, then 5, then every other person until we get back to the beginning. This means the first time round the people with numbers 1, 3, 5, 7 … will sit down, leaving the even numbers standing. On the second time round, and depending upon how many people there were in the original circle, the next sequence of people to sit down will be those either holding 2, 6, 10, 14 … or 4, 8, 12, 16 … Using this routine the problem continues until there is just one person left standing. Changing the number of people in the ring is the precursor to setting up the bigger problem, which is to work out the number left standing in relation to the number of people in the ring. Thus, if there are 27 people in the ring, number 22 will be left standing. If there are 19 people in the ring, number 6 will be left standing. Because the outcome of this problem is based upon the powers of 2, there are opportunities here for students to meet these numbers in another context.

There was one amusing occasion when I used this task at a Mathematics for Parents evening (see Chapter 14). Having carried out the procedure a couple of times I suggested, quite randomly, they try to fathom out what number would be left standing if there were 53 people in the ring. At the time I had not worked out the answer, so it was with much amusement when the answer produced was 42, the 'Ultimate Answer to the Ultimate Question of Life, the Universe and Everything' in Douglas Adams' *The Hitchhiker's Guide to the Galaxy*. This problem generates an interesting result and offers mathematical challenges to anyone who finds him or herself, for whatever reason, standing in a ring of people who each have a number and sit down at various times! Of course, once this problem has been sorted out, you might want to see what happen if every third person sits down …

Frogs and Fleas

The well-known Frogs problem would fit into the latter category and probably needs no explanation. However, just in case … The Frogs problem involves, say, four people with red hats and four people with green hats all sitting in a row.

There is an empty chair in the middle and the problem is to work out how they can all swap places using the following rules:

1 Either colour can slide to the adjacent, spare chair.
2 Either colour can hop over one other different colour to gain the spare chair.

This is a cracking good problem though there is also a computer version that can remove the possibility of a more socially inter-active experience for students, losing those lovely elements of working together while wearing silly hats. A development of working with the Frogs problem is to explore the sequence of moves when there are, say, 15 students on each side of the middle, empty chair. The solution to this problem could be practised as a performance, possibly for a school assembly. To facilitate this, students could be requested to turn up to school wearing one of two agreed colours, wearing green or yellow hats, or sporting red or blue noses.

   Another, perhaps slightly less-well-known, problem is called Fleas. Here a number of students in a line are to change their position from all sitting down to all standing up according to the following conditions:

1 Only one flea can make a move at one time.
2 A move is defined as a flea either standing up or sitting down.
3 In order for a flea to make a move the flea to their immediate left must be sitting down and anyone else further to their left must be standing up.
4 The flea on the far left (from the viewpoint of the other fleas) can move at any time.

Thus with five fleas A, B, C, D and E all sitting down, the first move could either be flea D or flea E to stand up. The problem is how to get everyone standing up using the minimum number of moves. Generalising the minimum amount of moves for any number of people presents a worthy challenge: indeed, the last time I used this problem was in 2010 with a Year 13 group in a school in Hong Kong. Given the general solution requires 'A' level-type knowledge, this was wholly appropriate.

Shifting places on a square grid

This idea is based upon eight students sitting on one each of nine chairs arranged in a three-by-three square with the top right-hand chair empty. The challenge is for the student sitting in the bottom left-hand chair to gain the top right-hand position, and is achieved by students moving horizontally or vertically to the empty adjacent chair. A record can be made of the moves made and what moves different students (counters) make.

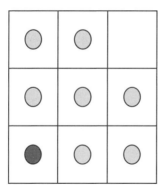

This problem can be extended to any sized square grid and even to rectangular grids. Again, this will provide extension work for some students.

The next idea is another problem based upon the binary number system.

From binary to denary

This is another standing up-/sitting down-type problem and is based upon five students sitting in a line, each having one of the values 16, 8, 4, 2 and 1 (i.e. the base 2 column headings). These can be written on big pieces of card or on hats. The task is to make all the base 10 values starting from 1, 2, 3 ... up to 31, with the appropriate students standing up when their number is required to contribute to each value. This can be a lot of fun particularly if, after any mistake occurs, students are asked to start again at number 1. The feeling of relief and the pleasure generated as the students successfully complete this task is always noteworthy.

An important outcome of such repetition is in helping to reveal the structure of the binary system. So the person holding number 1 stands up and sits down as alternate odd and even numbers are called, akin to a jack-in-the-box. The person holding number 2 stays standing for two consecutive numbers and sits for the next two numbers, and so on.

An extension to this task is to work in base negative 2, where the first five column headings are 16, −8, 4, −2 and 1. An important reason for using base negative 2 is so we can generate negative as well as positive numbers. In base negative 2, therefore, the value 17 will be written as 1001. With these column headings it becomes possible to generate all values from −10 to 21. Thus using base negative 2 provides students with a context for working with negative numbers. While we can never guarantee that common understandings will emerge from any task we offer, it is important for students to experience concepts in different contexts.

The next task is another of Peter's invention and is called Binary Twister.

Binary Twister

Write the numbers 1, 2, 4, 8 and 16 on five A4 pieces of coloured paper (all on the same colour). These are randomly laid out on the floor and students are invited to come forward and make a particular number using the numbers on the pieces of paper. They do this by placing a foot, hand, knee or any part of their anatomy on the pieces of paper they require.

For example, to make the number 11 requires 1, 2 and 8 so the student could stand with his or her feet on 1 and 2 and one hand on 8. No other part of the body can be in contact with the floor.

Students then suggest other numbers to make (31 is usually the most entertaining total as this clearly requires all 5 numbers).

Another task is to time how long it takes a student to make the numbers from 1 through to 31. Nimble footwork as well as good mental arithmetic is required.

To make things even more fun, introduce another set of numbers – 1, 2, 4, 8 and 16 – on another different colour of A4 paper, so now there are two students trying to make different totals similar to the game of twister. The students are very quick at choosing totals that require athleticism and good balance.

Cuisenaire arithmetic

This idea is based upon Cuisenaire Rods. These are coloured rods with a cross section of $1cm^2$ and of different lengths: the white rod is 1cm long, red 2cm, green 3cm, pink 4cm, yellow 5cm, turquoise 6cm, black 7cm, and orange is 10cm. Again, everybody sits in a ring of chairs and has a number from 1 upwards. Cuisenaire rods are distributed in the following way: Number 1 given a white rod (*w*), Number 2 a red rod (*r*), Number 3 a green (*g*), Number 4 a pink (*p*) and Number 5 a yellow (*y*). This colour sequence is repeated so Number 6 is given a white, Number 7 a red, and so on. While the rods are being given out I explain this particular 'world' of mathematics has only five colours and these are given out in the order *w*, *r*, *g*, *p* and *y*. I might ask students to tell me what colour they think they should be given. Very soon everyone has a coloured rod and a number.

There are several possible developments from here: one is to consider the set numbers given to students who hold the same-coloured rods. So, for example, after asking all those students holding a green rod to stand up, questions can be asked such as:

'What numbers between 50 and 60 would be green?'
'What number just under a 1000 would be green?'
'What do you notice about the green numbers?'

Such questions are likely to establish the pattern of the unit digits being a 3 or an 8.

As with the earlier 'Numbers in a ring' tasks, there is another opportunity to work on number patterns and to consider a linear sequence as a constant displacement from a specific multiplication table. Using the colours w, r, g, p and y, each person holding a yellow rod will be a multiple of five. So, by asking all those with a yellow rod to stand up and show their numbers, students will reveal numbers in the sequence $5n$. I usually write a vertical list on the board and ask all those holding, say, a green rod to stand and call out their numbers in order. This means the numbers 3, 8, 13, 18, 23 ... will be listed. Again, concepts of generalising linear sequences can be worked on as the following patterns emerge:

w	R	g	p	y
1	2	3	4	5
6	7	8	9	10
11	12	13	14	15
16	17	18	19	20
21	22	23	24	25
26	27	...	...	...
$5n - 4$	$5n - 3$	$5n - 2$	$5n - 1$	$5n$

The next task involves simple addition, and I ask two students to stand up, one with a green and the other a white rod. I ask them to hold up their number cards add them together and see what colour the answer is. Whichever green and white are used, the answer will always be pink, for example, 6 + 3, 1 + 13, 16 + 8 all produce an answer in the pink column. This is because we are operating in Modulo 5 and the equation $w + g = p$ can be written. Now other equations can be formed, using addition only at this stage. One challenge is to ask students to find all possible equations when two elements are added together. This idea can be developed to look at the addition of other pairs of colours and students can be asked to produce a two-way table:

+	*w*	*r*	*g*	*p*	*y*
w	r	g	p	y	w
r	g	p	y	w	r
g	p	y	w	r	g
p	y	w	r	g	p
y	w	r	g	p	y

A further development can be to look at what happens under multiplication.

×	*w*	*r*	*g*	*p*	*y*
w	w	r	g	p	y
r	r	p	w	g	y
g	g	w	p	r	y
p	p	g	r	w	y
y	y	y	y	y	y

We are now approaching Group Theory, which is usually the province of undergraduates. However, much younger students will be capable of exploring such structures and can, therefore, access the foundations for working on more complex areas of mathematics.

A further stage could be for students to consider what happens if we only have four colours instead of five: *w, r, g* and *p*. In this system the following number patterns emerge:

$$w \rightarrow 1, 5, 9, 13 \ldots r \rightarrow 2, 6, 10, 14 \ldots g \rightarrow 3, 7, 11, 15 \ldots$$
$$p \rightarrow 4, 8, 12, 16 \ldots$$

What happens to the addition and multiplication tables now under Modulo 4? Addition tables take on a predictable format. However, this is not the case for multiplication. If multiplication under Modulo 6, 7, 8, 9, 10 and so on is worked on, there is a splendid opportunity for students to produce a display out of their completed tables. Furthermore, if colours are used instead of symbols, this not only makes an attractive display, but the position of the colours also reveals underlying structures in a highly visual way. Students can look for general rules about the structures that exist within the tables, in particular seeking out similarities and differences.

All the ideas suggested so far can easily be used as starting points for further study and involve students working on tasks over several lessons. The following tasks are much shorter and could be carried out in a few minutes at any point in a lesson.

Subtracting a negative

Subtracting a negative value from something is certainly a highly abstract concept and I do not believe there is any one 'best' way of helping students to make sense of it. What I offer here are two approaches that might help:

Approach 1
Ask students to line up in order of size from smallest to tallest and give each person a card on which to write his or her measured height. The median height can now easily be shown as the person in the middle (or, if there is an even number, the value between the two people in the middle). Whatever this is, the idea is to give this measurement a value of zero, i.e. there is no difference between this measure and the median average.

Each student is asked to calculate his or her difference from the median (zero) and write this number as either a negative or a positive value on the reverse side of his or her card. At this point, everyone has his or her height written on one side and the difference from the median written on the other.

For the purpose of exemplification I shall assume that the median height for a class containing Jill and Jack is 155cm. If Jill is 161cm and Jack 147cm, a question such as 'What is the difference in height between Jill and Jack?' can be posed. The difference between 161 and 147 is clearly 14cm. When these cards are turned over, Jill will have the value $^+6$ on the reverse and Jack will have $^-8$. By using these numbers and turning the earlier question into a computation, we have $^+6 - {}^-8$, and this must also be equal to $^+14$. Students can pose further similar questions and there exists the possibility of holding a discussion about what is happening and why.

Approach 2

Another way of trying to demonstrate what happens when a negative value is subtracted from something is to give numbered playing cards to students. I explain two aspects about the task to the class. Firstly, a black playing card is a positive amount and a red playing card is a negative amount (being 'in the red'). Secondly, when a student is invited to stand at the front, the process of addition is taking place; when a student is asked to sit down, the process of subtraction is taking place. Now, if I ask a student with black 8 and another with a black 5 to come to the front, we have a total of 13, and I ask students to record this as $^+8 + {}^+5 = {}^+13$. If next a student with a red 4 comes to the front the total is now worth 9 and students write $^+13 + {}^-4 = {}^+9$. I can invite further students holding black and red cards to the front and at some point I am going to begin to ask students to sit down. I always start by asking a student with a black card to sit down to establish this is the process of subtraction. The crux of the task arises when a student holding a red card sits down.

For example, if we have the following collection of cards: black 8, black 5, red 4, black 2, red 5, black 9 the total at this point is $^+8 + {}^+5 + {}^-4 + {}^+2 + {}^-5 + {}^+9 = {}^+15$.

If the first black 8 is removed, the total goes down to $^+7$: mathematically we have $^+15 - {}^+8 = {}^+7$.

If a red 4 is removed, the total becomes $^+11$, thus an increase has occurred as an outcome of taking away a negative amount. Mathematically, the following has occurred: $^+7 - ^-4 = ^+11$.

Ultimately, the best we can do as teachers is to seek to provide students with a range of possibilities to explore why things work as they do. Such an approach is clearly different from one based upon giving students rules such as 'Two negatives make a positive' – unless, of course, you happen to be adding two negative values together!

Place value

I often wonder if the phrase 'place value' might usefully be replaced by the phrase 'the value of the place'. This may sound semantic. However, language is clearly important in making sense of anything. In order to help students make sense of what place value means, discussing what value any number takes when it is written in different places in our number system is worthwhile. This task is not intended to be a lengthy one and involves students lining themselves underneath the place value headings written on the board, for example, Th H T U . t h th

If zeros are then written in each of the positions this helps to show that the zeros are there all the time and we only need to record them when necessary. The idea is to allocate students one digit each, written on a piece of card, and for them to stand underneath one of the place value headings. Discussion can ensue about what number is being represented as digits stand under different column headings. This is clearly where the zeros become important and are necessary to make the digit 3 become 300, 4 become 40 or 5 become 0.5 when multiplying or dividing by powers of 10.

Loci

These ideas require a deal of space, so saving them for a sunny day and working outside the classroom adds to the interest. The main idea is for students to become locus points and position themselves according to certain rules. An old climbing rope or some bailer twine, a tape measure, some short stakes and a hammer are useful resources. Some rules might be given, including everyone standing ...

1 a fixed distance away from a stake in the ground;
2 an equal distance from two stakes in the ground;
3 a fixed distance away from a straight line (this is where the rope comes in handy);
4 on places that are equidistant between two lines meeting at an angle (again the rope can be used to make the angle, together with a stake knocked into the ground);
5 an equal distance away from a straight line and a point (stake in the ground);
6 so the sum of the distances away from two stakes in the ground is a constant. (This constant distance can be determined by joining together the two ends of a length of rope that also goes around both stakes.)

Loci produced by these situations are a circle, the perpendicular bisector, two parallel lines, the angle bisector, a parabola and an ellipse. Back in the classroom, students can construct these situations using a pencil, a pair of compasses and a straight edge. Understanding the loci created and learning their names is fundamental to this work.

This can be the precursor for further work on loci and a series of tasks is to consider what loci are created when the conditions of points, lines and circles are used in pairs. Choose pairs of 'conditions' – either two points, two lines, two circles, one point and one line, one point and one circle or one line and one circle. The problem is to find all the possible condition diagrams that can be made from all possible pairings. For example, with one point and one circle, the following four condition diagrams can be made:

✓ point outside the circle;
✓ point on the circumference of the circle;

✓ point inside the circle;

✓ point at the centre of the circle.

Of these four pairs of conditions, two of them are special cases (i.e. the point on circumference and point in the centre). The task now is to draw the loci of all the points that are equidistant between the point and the circle for each condition diagram. For example, the loci of the equidistant points for the condition diagram 'point inside the circle' (but not at the centre) is an ellipse.

Given the wide number of different condition diagrams, students can produce several, and there exists the possibility for much display work. As well as using drawing implements to produce constructions, there are also opportunities for students to use a dynamic geometry package as a way of enhancing their experience of loci.

Scale drawing

A task intended to cause students to engage with other concepts, particularly rotational symmetry and angle, is based upon car wheel trims – those things that fly off and can be found scattered on roadsides and hanging off hedgerows. Collecting a few of these as resources for the classroom can be useful. The idea is for students either to take photographs or make sketches of one or two of the more interesting wheel trim designs and to take just one approximate measurement. Using this information, students have to produce a half- or quarter-size scale drawing. Because of the rotational symmetry on many wheel trims, this task requires students to use protractors to replicate them. Of course, there will be some colleagues who rightly will not want anyone to go near their cars, and gaining permission to take one's class out into the car park to carry out such a task would be both politic and polite. Adorning a classroom wall with a number of spray-painted scale models of different car wheel trims can create an interesting display.

Teaching and the art of risk-taking

Teaching is a risky business and as such it is important to know why we may wish to use any idea that involves students not sitting behind their desks. As I mentioned at the beginning of this chapter, using such approaches is one way of providing students with variety in their mathematics lessons, and this can only be a good thing, especially if such variety is planned and carefully considered within schemes of work. Of course, taking risks can lead us into relatively unknown zones, and we cannot always envisage some of the pitfalls. Nor can we predict some of the benefits and the positive outcomes that occur when we enable students to see mathematics is not something that only happens while sitting behind a desk.

Using a range of teaching strategies is an important part of professional development. When I take a risk, I have to acknowledge that things won't happen as I had envisaged. However, I have got to try things out if I am going to be able to evaluate the usefulness of any strategy and be able to use an adapted version of an idea in future. If I want students to see their mathematics classroom as a place where different things happen, where variety is a touchstone and where fun and laughter form an important part of the culture of the classroom, I must be prepared to take some risks. I want my students to see their mathematics classroom as a place where relatively zany experiences occur, and through such occurrences they engage with mathematics that is interesting and challenging. Using people-math tasks requires the teacher to take all kinds of risks, and the more positive experiences we have as outcomes of the risks we take, the more varied our teaching styles and the more interesting places our classrooms can become.

A further key ingredient is identity. The development of one's identity as a teacher is connected to how interested we are in the job we do. Thinking about the nature of being a mathematics teacher, perhaps discussing with other teachers, through various networks or at conferences, how we seek to engage our students is all part of developing a teaching identity. There are issues here about discussing what learning mathematics involves and what this requires of students in order to be 'successful' learners. I would not wish to give an impression that teaching is an all-singing, all-dancing performance, yet there are times when I choose to exhibit larger-than-life ways of being. This, however, is not an act. The way I teach reflects who I am.

5

Using practical equipment in mathematics classrooms

Although mathematics is essentially a set of abstract concepts and the learning of mathematics is something that occurs in the mind, we need to have all kinds of experiences and stimuli to support this learning. These stimuli need to be a mixture of verbal, aural, visual and practical experiences to make the vital shift from the concrete to the abstract ... or, as Cundy and Rollett suggest:

> *Mathematics is often regarded as the bread and butter of science. If the butter is omitted, the result is indigestion, loss of appetite, or both. The purpose of this book is to suggest some ways of buttering the bread. The human mind can seldom accept completely abstract ideas; they must be derived from, or illustrated by, concrete examples. (1952, 13)*

The above quote is something I wish I had written! I use it here because it describes a key reason for using equipment to support the learning of mathematics. So why is practical equipment rarely used in some mathematics classrooms? Perhaps part of the answer lies in the fact that mathematics has traditionally been learnt sitting behind a desk with the teacher at the front coaxing out information, giving examples of how to do specific calculations, then providing questions on a worksheet or an exercise from a textbook. Furthermore, given students are not usually allowed to take manipulatives such as paper for paper-folding purposes, linking cubes, pinboards or pegboards with them into the examination room, there may seem little point in letting them use such equipment in preparation to take an examination. Whatever the reason, it seems using practical equipment in a mathematics classroom is fraught with dangers, adding a further dimension to an already highly complex set of circumstances.

However, the same students use practical equipment in other lessons, such as art, where a plethora of materials are used, in science and other technology-based subjects, and artefacts in history lessons. I am therefore at a loss to understand why the notion of using equipment in a mathematics lesson is sometimes seen as the devil incarnate, creating the potential for student misbehaviour, anarchy and civil unrest!

Sure, I have had the odd paper aeroplane sail through the air in lessons using paper-folding and have sometimes been shot at with a plastic gun constructed from linking cubes. On one occasion, an elastic band orchestra struck up when students were using geoboards. How I respond, how much of a meal or a big deal I make of such an event, is related to whether I see it as a challenge to my authority or whether I see such behaviour as a fairly natural part of life in a classroom. Moreover, because such events also occur with undergraduates and PGCE students, I am not at all surprised to see similar behaviours in young adolescents. This may sound like a good reason for not using practical equipment. However, I would be loathe to prevent students having opportunities to use manipulatives to make sense of mathematical concepts because a minority wish to test my levels of tolerance. Play is a necessary process, an important part of learning. In all kinds of situations we see just how far something will go, what the limits are and how flexible something is. We doodle and daydream, play around with ideas and knock things into shape. If this were not the case, some of the most significant inventions we take for granted could be lying dormant and many of the big ideas that affect our lives may have been left un-thought.

The case for using equipment

No equipment is imbued with the power to cause anyone to understand anything. This is equally true of a calculator or a sophisticated piece of computer software. How any equipment is used and the purposes behind its use are clearly important issues to consider at the planning stage of a lesson.

Similarly, some students will just not like being given equipment, seeing it as infantile. Offering students a choice of whether or not to use any equipment is, therefore, useful. This can easily be achieved. For example when I ask students to explore how many quadrilaterals they can find on a nine-dot-square grid, I always give them the choice of using a pinboard and an elastic band to help them with their work.

We cannot, however, say which learners are likely to receive the greatest benefit from using practical equipment, just as we cannot classify people, with any authority, as being strongly visual, auditory or kinaesthetic learners: this would be a false separation.

By providing students with equipment-based learning opportunities, we are certainly drawing upon two of the five senses: sight and touch. A fascinating comment I once received from an Eritrean teacher called Negasi, having worked with a nine-pin geoboard and an elastic band, was 'For the first time I can see mathematics.' Negasi's comment was particularly poignant as he had been totally blind since the age of six.

In this chapter I look at some potential uses of practical equipment in a mathematics classroom and at some strategies for implementation. In particular, I consider which mathematical concepts and specific skills I intend students to develop, practise, consolidate and understand. I begin with Tangrams, a set of seven shapes that form a square.

Tangrams

A problem I have frequently used is to give each student the seven pieces mixed up in an envelope and ask them to make a square. This in itself can be a challenge, yet because some will have previously met Tangrams they will not be new to everyone. Offering further tasks to challenge all students is therefore necessary. Such challenges could be to make other shapes – a parallelogram, a trapezium and a rectangle. While each of these

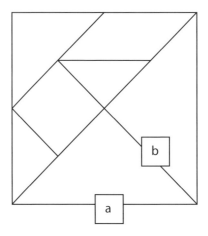

shapes clearly has the same area, they do not necessarily all have the same perimeter (I develop this below).

A further challenge is a problem I first came across in *Mathematics Teaching* 114. This is to try to find all 13 possible convex polygons. These are one triangle, six quadrilaterals, two pentagons and four hexagons. As shapes are produced, students could be asked to describe the symmetries of each one. Another problem could be to calculate the internal angle sum for each polygon, a task that requires students to sum angles that are multiples of 45°. This could lead to working on the connection between the number of sides of a polygon and its internal angle sum.

The next problem is based upon determining the perimeter of each shape. This problem would be more accessible to younger students if they are given lengths *a* and *b* (as marked in the diagram above) and use these to work out perimeters of the shapes they make. Such a task provides in-context opportunities for collecting like terms together and adding simple fractions such as halves and quarters. Post-Pythagorean students could be given the problem of working out perimeters if the length of the small square piece is 1. This provides opportunities to practise the use of surds and consolidate knowledge of Pythagoras' Theorem.

In the days before computers and digital cameras, I would mount a cine camera on a dexion frame and students would produce 16mm motion geometry pictures. The process was to take five single-frame shots of a shape, move a piece a short distance and take another five single frame shots, repeating this until they had transformed a square, say, into a triangle. The pre-stimulus for this was to show students the 'Dance Squared' film. This marvellous short film, produced by the Canadian Film Board, shows how a square can be dissected, transformed and reconstituted while dancing about the screen, all set to the most compelling piece of music you ever heard … Well, each to our own! Students subsequently produced short films based upon transformations.

The value of working with Tangrams is therefore in providing the potential for working on a variety of concepts: names and properties of shapes, area, perimeter, angle, algebraic coding, collecting like terms and calculation with surds. There are issues here about working in ways that connect mathematical concepts together.

Pegs and pegboards

Playing a game such as Four-in-a-Line can provide a stimulus for students to do some work on coordinates and equations of straight lines. One of the positive benefits of students producing lines from the games they play (in pairs) is they can work out each other's equations.

One way of using a pegboard to extend this problem is as follows. Hold up a board containing four pegs in a straight line about which its equation has or can be determined. Physically rotate the board about the centre point through 90°. Defining the point of rotation as the origin, students can be asked to work out how the equation of the line changes. We can ask what happens to the equation of the line when it is rotated 180° and 270°.

We can also 'flip' the board over, thereby producing reflections of the line in $y = 0$, $x = 0$, $y = x$ and $y = -x$. The challenge is to work out the equations of the new lines formed if we know the equation of the original line.

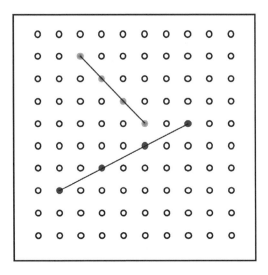

At this point students might be directed to explore combinations of rotations and reflections and (as in Chapter 4) work on Group Theory is not too far away.

Playing Four-in-a-square might be a starting point for work on vectors, area of squares and Pythagoras' Theorem (see Chapter 1). We can also make use of pegs and pegboards for working on problems such as Frogs and Fleas (see Chapter 4). In this way, students can use the equipment to work on such problems individually, if they find this preferable to wearing a silly hat and working in a group.

Pegs and pegboards can also be used for making sequences of shapes in order to explore patterns of growth leading to nth terms of sequences.

Using ATM 'beer' MATs

ATM MATs is a resource created by Adrian Pinel and produced by the Association of Teachers of Mathematics. This resource is a set of shapes based mainly upon regular polygons with a fixed edge length. They are made from material similar to that of beer mats and can be used for 2D or 3D work.

Creating 2D tessellations

There are, of course, only three regular tessellations and these are those made using equilateral triangles, squares and regular hexagons. Finding the complete set of semi-regular tessellations is much more interesting and challenging as these are made from combinations of polygons (of side lengths 3, 4, 6, 8 and 12). The ATM MATs are a perfect resource for such an exploration and the diagram below shows one such semi-regular tessellation using squares and octagons.

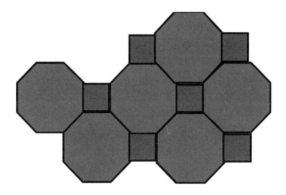

Once such a design has been made students can calculate internal angles. Thus by choosing any point on the above tessellation where shapes meet, there are always two octagons and one square.

Creating 3D models

To make 3D polyhedra, Copydex glue is essential to stick the MATs together to form solids. Not only is this glue quick drying, but solids can also be recycled, especially if the glue is applied sparingly in the first instance. For construction purposes MATs are easily stuck together using the tiniest smear of glue.

Making 3D models such as the Platonic and Archimedean solids can provide students with much interest. The five Platonic solids (or regular polyhedra) are the tetrahedron, the hexahedron (or the cube), the octahedron, the dodecahedron and the icosahedron. Given there are two infinite sets and one finite set of

Archimedean solids, there will be plenty to go at! Also see *100+ Ideas for Teaching Mathematics*, (2005, pp. 105–109). My preferred starting point is to have equilateral triangle and square MATs only in circulation, so the first task is to produce solids made only of triangles, squares, or combinations of both. Restricting students to using these shapes generates a lot of solids and these can be explored before other shapes are introduced. An interesting shape to emerge is the cuboctahedron, which, as its name suggests, is made from six square and eight equilateral triangle MATs. A continuation task is to consider Euler's Rule: the relationship between faces (F), vertices (V) and edges (E) for any polyhedron.

A central aspect of learning mathematics is for students to explore structure, and work based upon polyhedra provides many such opportunities. However, a further outcome of model making is to enhance the classroom environment. Principally, I want students to engage with the resources first-hand and see for themselves something of the intrigue and the beauty of mathematics.

Euler and truncations

Exploring Euler's relationship is a fairly 'closed' problem. An extension is to explore truncations of solids, which are solids made by slicing off vertices of polyhedra in two different ways. One is to truncate anywhere between each vertex and the mid-point of corresponding edges. The other is to truncate at the mid-point of each edge. So, for each Platonic solid, other solids can be made. Looking for connections between F, V and E for each Platonic solid and their truncations opens up opportunities for students to use symbols to describe what happens. The cuboctahedron emerges as an interesting solid as it is created by truncating both the cube and the octahedron at the mid-point of the edges.

Duals of polyhedra

A dual is produced by joining together the centre point of each face of a solid (we can also form duals of tessellations made from 2D polygons). With Platonic solids, the tetrahedron is a self-dual. The dual of the cube is the octahedron and vice versa. The dual of the dodecahedron is the icosahedron and vice versa. The problem becomes more challenging when duals of Archimedean solids are considered. This task would be a challenge at Key Stage 4 and Key Stage 5.

Finding all the deltahedra

Another interesting problem is to find all the possible deltahedra. These are convex polyhedra made only from equilateral triangle faces, forming a finite set of solids. Asking students to explore what these solids are is a significant challenge. This problem can lead to students classifying the solids according to how many faces meet at each vertex. So, for example, three of the possible deltahedra are the tetrahedron, the octahedron and the icosahedron, which have three, four and five faces respectively meeting at each vertex. The other deltahedra are made from combinations of three, four and five faces meeting at vertices.

More problems

More complex problems, some of which could challenge under-graduate students, are:

✓ calculating the surface areas and volumes of polyhedra;
✓ calculating the volumes of the inscribed and circumscribed spheres of polyhedra;
✓ calculating the dimensions of a cuboid such that when it is sliced through one of its planes of symmetry the resulting

cuboid is similar to the original (the solution to the equivalent problem in 2D is when a sheet of A4 paper is cut in half to A5);
✓ calculating the dihedral (or the 'solid' angles) of polyhedra.

Circular geoboards

Circular geoboards have either an odd number of pins or an even number; each has a pin at the centre. Problems based upon finding triangles and quadrilaterals provide students with another context for naming and classifying shapes they make. Students can also create a systematic method to prove they have found them all.

Angles can be calculated and one way to achieve this is to use the centre pin as a 'construction' point. So with a nine-pin (plus one at the centre) geoboard, the smallest angle formed at the centre is 40°. The circular geoboard is also an excellent piece of equipment for working on circle theorems:

✓ opposite angles of cyclic quadrilaterals summing to 180°;
✓ angles at the circumference subtended from a common chord being equal;
✓ the angle at the centre being twice the angle at the circumference.

With a ten-pin (plus one at the centre) geoboard, diameters can be formed between opposite pairs of pins, and this can lead students towards the theorem of angles at the circumference of a circle, subtended from a diameter, being 90°.

A real-life circular geoboard

Asking 10 students to sit as equally spaced as possible in a circle and pass round a ball of string usually creates an interesting start to a lesson. The first person wraps one end of the string around a finger and throws the ball to another person a fixed number of spaces away. This person pulls the string tight, wraps it around a finger and passes the ball to another person. So, with 10 people in the circle, various outcomes occur, depending upon the add rule used:

Rule	Outcome
+1	Decagon
+2	Pentagon
+3	10-pointed star
+4	5-pointed star
+5	Straight line
+6	5-pointed star
+7	10-pointed star
+8	Pentagon
+9	Decagon

The symmetry here is likely to emerge and students can explain why this occurs. Further tasks and problems, each of which may lead to generalities, are:

- ✓ exploring the number of times the ball passes the starting point knowing the number of people in the circle and the pass rule;
- ✓ changing the number of people in the starting circle;
- ✓ seeing what happens when the number of people in the circle share a common factor with the size of the add rule;
- ✓ seeing what happens when there is a prime number of people in the ring;
- ✓ exploring a pair of add rules, e.g. + 2 followed by + 3 with 10 people in the circle a rectangle is formed;
- ✓ calculating the total length of string for each shape made;
- ✓ calculating the angles of shapes formed at the circumference.

Paper-folding

There are dozens of paper-folding tasks to enable students to work on a range of concepts. I begin this section with what do with scrap pieces of card and sugar paper that are too big to throw away – you know, those pieces of card where students have automatically cut a shape right out of the middle, leaving the remainder of the card seemingly redundant!

Some centres of a triangle

Using scrap card students draw and cut out acute-angled, right-angled and obtuse-angled triangles. They are now in a position to explore what happens when they fold the sides of triangles in half. This creates perpendicular bisectors where each fold line meets at a single point, the centre of the circumscribed circle. Whether the triangle has three acute angles, an obtuse angle or a right angle will determine whether the meeting point is inside, outside or on the edge of the hypotenuse of the triangle. In the latter case students are only a few steps away from seeing the hypotenuse as the diagonal of a circle. As such, the theorem of a diameter subtending a 90° angle at the circumference is close to realization.

A similar task is to fold each angle in half to form the angle bisectors: these lines meet at a point, the centre of the inscribed circle.

Finding the centroid of a triangle by folding or drawing the mid-point of each edge to the opposite angle is a further task. Checking the accuracy of this can be done by balancing the triangle on a pencil at this point.

To begin to make sense of the concept of where this centre point (centroid) is, students could measure the distances from the mid-point of each side to the centre of mass and from the centre of mass to each angle and recognise the 1:2 ratio. Indeed, this is a useful starting point for older students to develop a vector proof.

A further problem is to explore what happens when the perpendicular bisectors of quadrilaterals are drawn. With asymmetrical quadrilaterals, each pair of bisectors will meet at a point, and these four points will produce the corners of another quadrilateral. Exploring the relationship between the original and the new quadrilateral will be a fine challenge: using interactive geometry software would be useful here.

These paper-folding tasks can also be replicated in a more traditional manner using a pencil, a pair of compasses and a straight edge. All of these modes of working bring particular aspects of geometry to students' attention. One is not better than another – just different – and as such it is useful for all students to experience all these ways of working.

More paper-folding

If I had a penny for every piece of A4 paper I have guillotined down to A5 and A6, into squares and into strips, I would be a very rich person! As it is, I have been enriched by the many lessons and sessions I have taught using the spoils of a guillotine. A range of shapes can be formed from the following starting point.

Take an A6 piece of paper and fold it once, so a trapezium with two right angles, a 45° and a 135° angle is formed:

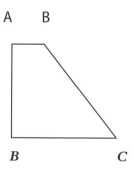

We can ask questions about what properties the shape has. Students can make beautiful tiling displays using brightly coloured paper and sticking the folded shapes on to sugar paper: in this case I would probably cut the paper down to A7.

The tiling pattern below is formed by rotation and translation.

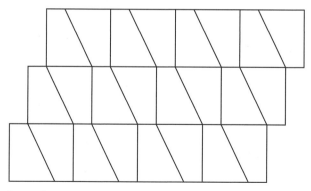

By making the same shape from two different sizes, say A5 and A7, some work on scale factors and centres of enlargement, including negative enlargements, is viable if students draw ray lines connecting corresponding points to observe how these lines meet at a common point, the centre of enlargement.

By folding down corner A a kite is produced; an interesting feature is that it looks much more kite-like once it is turned over on to the unfolded side of the paper.

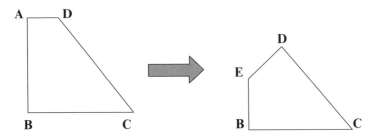

Another feature is that because the lengths of the original trapezium AB, BC, CD and DA are 1, $\sqrt{2}$, $\sqrt{2}$ and ($\sqrt{2} - 1$) respectively, the perimeter of the kite is ... well, it is a lovely problem to work on with a very satisfying result!

Returning to the trapezium (ABCD), there is a range of shapes that can be created by one or two further folds, such as a rhombus, an isosceles trapezium and another kite, this one having 45°, 112.5°, 112.5° and 90° angles.

The equipment I have written about in this chapter or refer to elsewhere in this book requires the department to build up a stock of resources that is affordable and accessible. Stocks of equipment might be stored either in designated mathematics rooms or centrally. Having any resource readily available (and this is particularly true for computers and graphical calculators) means being able to make use of them in unanticipated ways. This is important, as we cannot predict when a particular resource may suddenly become useful. Students need access to lots of resources: different grid papers, string, card, sugar paper, glue, scissors, pairs of compasses, rulers, protractors, linking cubes, ATM MATs, geoboards, pegs and pegboards, Cuisenaire rods, empty boxes of cornflakes, dice, cards, dominoes, clinometres, metre sticks, crayons ... all in the name of learning mathematics.

6

Mental mathematics

From age 11 to 16 I worked on a milk round. I remember the enjoyment I took from calculating customers' milk bills, frequently amazing them with the speed at which I did this. At 18 I worked as a waiter at the Burnley Cabaret Club, easily transferring my mental arithmetic skills from milk to alcohol sales. I also do the Kakuro puzzle on the back of the *Guardian 2* (arithmetically, so much more interesting than Suduko). These mental activities are something I do as simple mind-challenges and for whatever reason I gain small amounts of pleasure from carrying out mental calculations.

For some people, 'mental arithmetic' is one of the scariest phrases in the English language. This is unsurprising, given the amount of pressure felt by some young children in some classrooms to carry out calculations in their heads, at speed, against the clock. This increased focus on children carrying out calculations both mentally and with pencil and paper, in contrast to reaching for a calculator, is significant and important. It is significant in terms of raising the debate about the use of calculators in classrooms and perceptions of the impact calculators have upon children's learning. It is important because mental mathematics impacts significantly upon children's confidence with mathematics and their self-esteem as learners. Confidence breeds competence and self-esteem is crucial in personal development. If children are to perceive mathematics as something they 'can do' and can take pleasure from, then learning to solve problems mentally is an important aspect of raising self-esteem.

Working with some Key Stage 3 students on a one-to-one programme I met this issue of the connection between confidence, competence and self-esteem first hand. My approach was to offer students puzzles through which they would need to engage with mental arithmetic. It became clear that most of them relied upon finger-counting when faced with the most simple of calculations. I felt this reliance upon finger-counting slowed the students down to the point where they had forgotten the purpose for doing the calculation in the first place. Furthermore once they had achieved an answer they did not know whether it was correct as they had no way of checking if they had miscounted. A particularly 'sad' example was when one student needed to calculate 15 + 8. He immediately counted on his fingers, starting at 15, and proceeded to count on another 8. I asked him whether he knew of another way of adding 8 to something and he replied he could 'add on 10 and ... [after a few seconds' pause] take away two'. I suggested he tried this method, expecting him to compute fifteen plus ten is twenty five in his head. However, what actually happened was he again counted on his fingers from 15 up to 25. What was particularly poignant about this event was the student's inability to mentally add on 10 to something: it appeared he had no confidence to do anything other than finger-count.

This begs a significant and important issue – how learners are enabled to develop their powers of performing mental calculations without continually relying upon manipulatives such as fingers, blocks, bricks (including Cuisenaire and Diene's apparatus) number lines, charts and calculators. I am a firm believer in the use of concrete materials such as Cuisenaire, Diene's apparatus and linking cubes. However, the use of such manipulatives to support learning must be balanced with the use of mental approaches. It is not a case of one or the other it is the value of both.

In Chapter 1 I discussed 'the five-ness of 5' when working with Early Years Foundation Stage (EYFS) children several years ago and how children needed to recognise how numbers exist in lots of different contexts. Of course, the number doesn't have to be 5. The teacher might choose a number for the week. Consequently display work and/or a table might be used for a collection of items that pertain to the chosen number. Sticking to 5 for now, older pupils could be asked questions such as:

✓ How long would it take you to run 500 metres?

✓ Use a map to find some places which are 5 miles away from your school.

✓ Explain why 5 is a prime number.

✓ Find ways of making the answer 5 using square numbers, e.g.
$1^2 + 2^2 = 5$, $3^2 - 2^2 = 5$, $5^2 - 4^2 - 2^2 = 5$

✓ Make up five really hard questions so the answer is always 5.

✓ Explain why 5 is a number in the Fibonacci Sequence.

✓ The five 5s problem: see if you can make answers using five 5s. We can use addition, subtraction, multiplication, division, and place value (i.e. 55). We may also use 5!, which is a shorthand way of writing 5x4x3x2x1. For example, to make the answer of 8 we could have $(5! - 55) \div 5 - 5$.

Developing mental strategies to work with numbers is a key issue. I am sure many of us will recognise the amazing speed at which dart players carry out computations: developing such a facility with numbers is all part of enhancing the skill and precision of throwing darts. This is possibly because the longer a player has to take between throwing each dart the more disrupted their automated flow becomes. Context and motivation play significant roles here.

However, there are too many adults prepared to voice an inability to do mathematics (unlike having difficulties with reading or writing), sometimes as a measure of kudos. This is possibly a reflection upon how some may have experienced school mathematics. The fear some adults have and the kind of memories some have about how they were taught mathematics is a problem that must be recognised if some children, of current and future generations, are to experience a lesser fear.

So, what do mathematics lessons look, feel and sound like?

What expectations or perceptions do students have about mathematics lessons? How do mathematics lessons look, feel and sound? In what ways do students come to learn to behave, mathematically? In part, answers to these questions will be influenced by individual teacher's expectations together with the culture he or she seeks to create within the classroom.

If students expect to carry out calculations mentally in a mathematics lesson, so over time they come to 'know' about facts and routines, this is a reasonable expectation to have. However, we cannot expect all children to be able to carry out calculations at the same speed while the clock is ticking. They must be encouraged to play around with numbers, to manipulate them, to see how numbers are connected to other numbers, to see how the same numbers exist in a wide range of different situations. They need to 'know' about mathematical calculations in gentle, supportive, non-competitive ways. A typical example of coming to 'know' about mathematics relies upon students becoming confident, over time, about certain facts. There are many facts about numbers that students will benefit from by being able to recognise and come to know about, without having to stop to work out.

Take the number 13, for instance:

- ✓ 13 is the sum of two squares ($2^2 + 3^2$).
- ✓ 13 is a prime number.
- ✓ 13 is a number in the Fibonacci sequence.
- ✓ 13 is the square root of 169.
- ✓ 13 is the number of cards in a suit in a pack of cards.

Further, lesser-known facts about the number 13 are:

- ✓ 13 (using four 4s) is $44/4 + \sqrt{4}$.
- ✓ 13 in base three is 111.
- ✓ 13 is the hypotenuse of a 5, 12, 13 triangle, which itself is a Pythagorean triple.

Of course, the idea could be reversed, i.e. 'If the answer is 13, what could the question be?' Helping students to establish a working knowledge about number facts so they see the different properties numbers have in different contexts and different sequences is a key aspect of coming to know about numbers and building confidence.

Doing calculations mentally and written are both important. Mental mathematics, however, is all too strongly associated with numerical calculations often carried out at a speed determined by someone else, either the teacher or, with regard to mental tests, by a government quango via national tests.

Whilst being able to carry out such calculations is undeniably important, it is also important to recognise that 'in the real world' if we need to do a calculation we do not have someone standing over us with a stopwatch. In the real world we may make an estimate, we may ask somebody else or we may consult the chart in the DIY store. If we need an accurate answer we may choose to use a calculator perhaps on a mobile phone. We may decide to carry out the calculation later when we have more time to think about it. Of course, many children enjoy the challenge of working out answers to mental arithmetic questions at speed. However, danger lies in children comparing themselves with each other, and this can be particularly difficult for children who need more time to work something out in order to arrive at the required answers. In such situations the competitive nature of a mental arithmetic test might well offer 'success' to those children who usually answer most questions correctly, however we must also consider the impact on those children who do not.

Children can be encouraged to share methods they use, help one another construct mental methods and support each other in the refinement of calculation methods. Such approaches are currently used in some schools for the greater benefit of students. There is a range of tasks that can be introduced, such as imagining number lines, number grids and conceptions of infinity. Peter Lacey's article 'Using Geometric Images of Number to Teach Mental Addition and Subtraction' in *Mathematics Teaching* 163 (1998) offers a rich vein of mental arithmetic tasks.

An aspect of mental mathematics that is not given the same degree of time of attention, however, is geometric imagery. This has much to offer. Balancing activities between arithmetical and geometrical work will provide students with other perspectives on mental mathematics. The following ideas therefore consider mental mathematics as mind-imagery, taking a geometrical perspective.

Mathematics and imagination

As discussed on p. 4, 'Mathematics from 5 to 16' has one of its aims as 'imagination, initiative and flexibility of mind in mathematics'. The next section develops the power of the imagination; of mathematics in the mind. I begin with a mental activity designed to turn a square into a circle.

This idea is something I frequently use with groups, sometimes as a starter task for trigonometry. I invite students to close their eyes and ask them to create pictures in their heads. Okay, here goes – close your eyes. No, don't … You won't be able to read the next bit! Just imagine you have your eyes closed and are responding to the following:

1 Imagine a square.
2 Shrink it, enlarge it, decide upon its colour.
3 Place your imaginary square on your forehead and make sure you can see its edges.
4 Now draw in the two diagonals of the square.
5 Look at the point where these diagonals meet and place a drawing pin (ouch).
6 Now start turning the square anti-clockwise, very slowly about the drawing pin.
7 Now speed up the rotation, go faster and faster.
8 Rotate even faster, as fast, as fast as possible …
9 Stop, open your eyes.

What did you see? With a bit of imagination it is possible to turn a square into a circle.

To use this imagining as a starter task for trigonometry, half the length of the diagonal becomes the rotating arm and needs to be placed on a coordinate grid, where the origin is the centre of rotation. We subsequently draw up cosine and sine tables, which are the horizontal and vertical coordinates that describe the position of the end of the rotating arm (see Ollerton and Watson 2001, 113–15).

Some other questions we might ask in order to progress to

work on other concepts relating to pi, circumference, area, percentage increase and loci are:

✓ How is the circle related to the square?

✓ How does the perimeter of the square compare to the circumference of the circle?

✓ What is the percentage increase of the perimeter of the square to the circumference of the circle?

✓ How does the area of the square compare to the area of the circle?

✓ Suppose the drawing pin is placed in the corner of the original square. What happens now as the square is rotated?

✓ Suppose the drawing pin is placed halfway along the edge of the square. What happens now?

✓ Suppose I rotate the square about one of its corners and trace out two concentric circles formed by an adjacent corner and the opposite corner of the square. What is the circumference and area of each circle?

✓ Suppose we rotate two concentric squares where one square is half the edge length of the other?

There are so many questions that might be used either as a starting point for certain concepts or as an extension task as concepts begin to become embedded in students' mathematical development. While different students will be able to hold different amounts of information in their heads, there needs to be a point in proceedings where discussion about what different students see turns into a sketch. This change of approach to the task is valuable in terms of adding variety to students' mathematical experience. The unanswerable question is when the mathematics in students' heads needs to become diagrams on pieces of paper. This, of course, depends upon teachers' professional decision-making skills.

Intersecting circles

This task involves asking students to imagine two circles of the same size moving towards each other along a line that joins the centres of the circles together.

1 Imagine two circles of the same size.
2 At the beginning the circles are not overlapping.
3 Now imagine a line joining the centres of the circle.
4 Move the circles towards each other so the centres stay on the line just drawn.
5 When the two circles touch each other make them move very slowly.
6 When they just overlap, stop, and draw dots at the points where the circles intersect.
7 Form a shape by joining lines from the centre of each circle to these intersection points.
8 Start the circles moving again so the centres come closer together.
9 Stop and again join lines from the centres of the circles to the points of intersection.

One might use the image of an elastic band around the four points, so describing a more dynamic image. Questions can be asked about the shapes formed, e.g. how their perimeters compare, how their areas compare and what happens when circles of different sizes move towards each other (thus producing kites instead of rhombuses). Trying to answer questions about perimeter and area again requires students to record what they saw and, in the first instance, to consider particular cases, given the radii of the circles and the distance between the centres.

Slicing a square

This mental imagery task is about creating shapes from two isosceles right-angled triangles (IRATs) formed by slicing a square down one of its diagonals.

1 Imagine a square with opposite pairs of sides sitting horizontally and vertically on your forehead.
2 Slice the square down the diagonal from top left-hand to bottom right-hand corner. (At this point students can be asked

to say what shapes they have formed in order to establish what properties the shapes have and what sizes the angles are.)

3 You are going to move the triangle on the right hand side and keep the other one still. Imagine the left-side triangle is red and the triangle on the right is blue. Slide the blue triangle down the diagonal until the top left-hand corner is just touching the bottom right-hand corner of the red triangle. Now slide the blue triangle along the bottom edge of the red triangle until the two edges are joined together.

4 What shape is now formed?

5 Now slide the blue triangle horizontally to the left until the two 90° angles are just touching at a point. Now rotate the blue triangle clockwise about this point through an angle of 90° until the blue triangle touches the red triangle edge to edge.

6 What shape is now formed?

Within this sequence of movements all the shapes that can be formed by joining two IRATs full edge to full edge will have been made. This could be a precursor to a systematic exploration of the shapes formed by joining three or four IRATs.

Moving from mental imagery to recording could be a paired or small group task. Students might be given the brief of finding out as much information as possible about the shapes formed and preparing a poster to present what they have found.

Hot seating and the Great Dodecahedron

The final task in this section is one that requires a certain resource (published by Tarquin) – 'The Great Dodecahedron' poster, a beautiful picture printed in six colours.

The strategy I use is sometimes referred to as 'hot seating'. I arrange the class in a couple of arcs around the board with the poster displayed on the board. Next to it is an empty seat. This is the hot seat, and students are invited to come and sit upon it when they have something to say about the poster to the rest of the class. I implement a 'no pointing' rule, insisting that once in the hot seat students literally have to sit on their hands. Thus they have to describe what they see without being able to draw hand pictures or point to the poster.

This task always generates a great deal of fun and laughter as students in the hot seat go through mental contortions to explain to others what they can see. Because of the complexity of the poster and the wide range of both 2D and 3D shapes that can be seen, there can be many possible contributions. Usually after the poster has been discussed for 15 or 20 minutes or when contributions appear to have dried up I ask the question: 'So, do you think you know a lot about this picture?' Because students are usually wise to such rhetorical or loaded questions, they know something else is about to happen ... and they are quite right!

I take the poster down and give everyone an ATM hexagon MAT. Using this as an outline (which is the 2D outline of the shape on the poster) I ask them to try to replicate what they have discussed and seen. This is frequently met with 'anguished' moans: however, having got over the initial shock, students tend to beaver away at the task, which opens up opportunities for paired or small group discussion about what the picture looked like. By the end of a lesson there are various drawings and students are always keen to have a second look at the poster to check out the accuracy of their work.

The ideas I have described in this section might be used as stimuli for 'one-off' lessons or as starting points for more extensive pieces of mathematics. The important issue is variety: to offer students tasks that require the use of different skills and aptitudes and to work in different ways. Underpinning such tasks is the value of mental imagery, discussion and the power of enjoyment. When learners see mathematics as something to be embraced, something they can enjoy and play around with, they are less likely to recoil in fear when they find other aspects of mathematics difficult and challenging. Reducing the fear of mathematics and replacing it with fun and enjoyment is a sizable and wholly desirable challenge. As I have commented elsewhere, whilst enjoyment is desirable, the greatest joy arises through understanding mathematics – an outcome of learners becoming more mathematically savvy and more confident to have a go.

PART 3

7

Mathematics across the curriculum

This chapter is about places where mathematics occurs in other contexts beyond investigations of 'pure' mathematical situations. I look at connections between mathematics and history, art and dance and consider examples of other places where mathematics naturally exists.

How many times have we heard a student exclaim something such as 'Why are we writing in a maths lesson? That's what we do in English!' Behind such a statement lies a worrying feature of our secondary education system, where subject boundaries are largely fixed by timetables where students experience different subjects in different doses with different teachers in different classrooms. It is hardly surprising how students, therefore, section off their learning into discrete packages. A worrying feature is some students' seeming inability to transfer knowledge learnt in one subject area to another. Indeed, transferring learning within the same subject is often difficult at times.

Enabling students to transfer knowledge and skills is a necessary though complex business and no amount of seeking to remind students of the knowledge they possess or should possess is likely to enable the process. Transfer of knowledge and skills happens at best intuitively, automatically and consequentially. An excellent example occurred when I was working recently alongside Sherrilee, a newly qualified primary school teacher.

Sherrilee's Year 4 class had been studying life in Viking times and she wanted her pupils to have a practical mathematics/cross-curricular experience based upon making 2D and 3D scale drawings and models. She organised her class to work in four mixed-ability groups to measure and mark out, on the school yard, the floor plan of a typical Viking habitation, using a given scale of 1:50. This took place before a lunch break and after lunch she asked her pupils to make life-size 3D models of some furniture and a fire hearth based upon a scale drawing.

I was interested in the way Sherrilee organised her teaching and how strategic she was at standing back, intervening only when pupils requested support. This took a degree of professional nerve, recognising that were she to intervene too soon this could potentially prevent pupils from making their own choices and decisions, key characteristics of a problem-solving classroom. Sherrilee provided the class with a range of materials including straws, newspapers, sugar paper, string, scissors and sticky tape, informing her pupils that they must decide what materials they needed. Meanwhile, I performed the roles of storekeeper and general dogsbody, such as distributing tape when requested. In the final ten or so minutes of the lesson, after the most amazing tidying-up process I have ever seen, Sherrilee asked each group or sub-group to present their completed or part-finished models to the rest of the class. In particular, Sherrilee asked pupils to explain something they were pleased about and something they thought they might do better on another occasion – teacher assessment and self-assessment in action here in a most powerful and purposeful way.

My analysis of this activity, in terms of transfer of knowledge and skills, was of pupils being enabled to use and apply existing knowledge and skills and when they needed to ask questions or seek guidance they felt confident to do so. Essentially, pupils were actively involved in the tasks provided and basically just got on with it, making decisions as and when the need arose. Of course, the lesson had been well planned with resources prepared. The main feature, however, was Sherrilee's pedagogy, which was based upon wanting her pupils to:

✓ make decisions and be problem-solvers;
✓ make choices;
✓ work collaboratively;
✓ engage with mathematics in a cross-curricular way;
✓ evaluate the work they had done;
✓ communicate this evaluation to the rest of the class.

Mathematics and Art

There are a multitude of connections between art and mathematics, many geometric by nature. There exists numerical connections, particularly through the Golden Ratio, which itself is strongly connected with geometry. So, for example, in a regular pentagon the ratio of the length of a diagonal to the length of the side is 1.62 (to two decimal places), and this is an approximation to the Golden Ratio. It is worth stating at this point that just because such connections exist I am not advocating that the art teacher should turn an art lesson into a mathematics lesson or vice-versa.

However, if we are aware connections exist, then helping students become similarly aware is one way of providing them with a coherent, joined-up education. For the art teacher, therefore, to give some mention, where appropriate, to mathematical connections, and for the mathematics teacher to give value to the aesthetic aspects of mathematics, can only enhance students' overall learning experience.

Any work involving tessellation and tiling designs can be aligned to art, and the work of the Dutch artist M. C. Escher provides classic examples of this interface. Exploring which shapes form regular and semi-regular tessellations, classifying a tessellation, considering sizes of angles of the shapes involved and asking questions about whether a tessellation is based upon reflections, rotations, translations and/or combinations of these may be considered as more mathematical. However, providing students with opportunities to make shapes and 'play' with tessellations and tiling designs is less distinguishable from art, while simultaneously being an important precursor to further mathematical investigation.

Tiling quadrilaterals using vectors

This idea starts by drawing any quadrilateral with vertices on the intersection points of a square grid. The next step is to describe the shape using vectors by defining each of the four line segments. For example, using the quadrilateral below, we have:

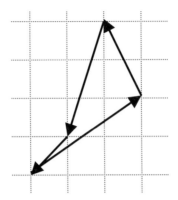

The vectors (moving clockwise around the shape) are:

$$\binom{3}{2} \quad \binom{^-1}{2} \quad \binom{^-1}{^-3} \quad \binom{^-1}{^-1}$$

The arrows show how adjacent pairs of vectors are connected. The first and the last vectors, as described above, are also adjacent.

Checking the sum of these vectors is $\binom{0}{0}$ may be useful.

Once these vectors have been established the idea is to draw line segments on a grid determined by the vectors. The rule for drawing these is to start with any vector, draw the line, then move to either adjacent vector and draw a second line. Continue this process, sometimes going over a line already drawn, and after 20 or so lines have been drawn, the tessellation pattern should become clear. Because any quadrilateral will tessellate, this vector method will also produce a tiling design, made from a combination of translations and rotations of the shape used. Tessellating triangles using this vector method will be a simpler process, but the designs produced are not nearly as interesting as those based upon quadrilaterals.

We may want students to explore the duals of tessellations. This is where the 'centre' points of shapes in a tessellation are joined together with the new lines crossing just one arc of the original tessellation. A simple example is to consider a tessellation of equilateral triangles; the dual is a tessellation of regular hexagons. Looking for connections between a tessellation and its dual is a challenging problem, particularly with semi-regular tessellations. A further problem using dual tessellations is described in the ATM publication *Learning and Teaching Mathematics without a Textbook* (2002, 19–21).

An Eritrean tiling design

The tile below, made from a combination of non-regular pentagons and kites, is the basis of a pavement design on Liberation Avenue in Asmara, Eritrea.

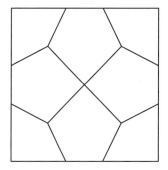

The first weekend I was in Asmara I was strolling around the city with two colleagues, Sheila and Helen, and noticed the tiling design on the pavement. It was a design I had never seen before and I was interested in the geometry of the tile. I begged a piece of paper from Helen, got down on my knees and began to trace the outline of the tile. Quite quickly a small group of Eritreans gathered around to see what was happening while my colleagues pretended not to be with me. As I got more excited Sheila asked why not take a photograph of the design rather than scrabbling around on the pavement, a copy of which appears on the front cover of the aforementioned ATM publication.

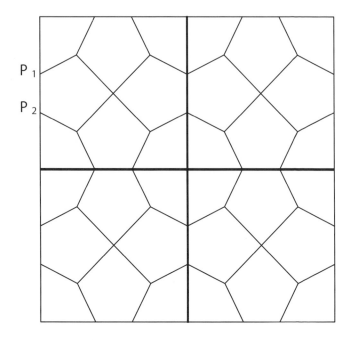

Exploring the geometry of this tile I noticed that by extending the two sides of the pentagon starting from points P1 and P2 they go to opposite corners of the square. One angle in each pentagon P1 P2 is 90° and the other four angles are equal (112.5°). This makes the obtuse angle of each kite 135°. I also explored the dual of this design and this produced a further interesting design made up of squares, triangles and an isosceles trapezium.

Whether this design is used as a stimulus for an art, mathematics or even a geography lesson is largely irrelevant. What is important is recognizing the cross-curricular possibilities and, therefore, the value of departments communicating with one another about common ideas and the possibility of making connections between disciplines explicitly to students.

Mathematics and Dance

Dance and mathematics was an idea I first met at the Easter 2009 ATM conference held at Swansea at a session run by

Anne Watson and Nichola Clarke, which proved sensational. Subsequently, I have offered a slightly adapted version during CPD events with teachers and trainee teachers. I call the idea 'The Dance of the Divisors' and it works as follows. I ask eleven other people to join me and stand in a circle, this arrangement being twelve ones, or 1×12. All we have to do now is to link hands in the circle and we collectively become one twelve, or 12×1. Pairing-up forms six groups of two, or 2×6. Moving into groups of threes or fours produces 3×4 or 4×3 respectively. The challenge is to create a dance routine where the dancers transform themselves gracefully into different groups, intentionally, as smoothly and as ordered as possible. Of course there are lots of opportunities to consider issues of rotations and reflections and how different-sized groups form and reform as the dance progresses. There is also an issue of how the dance can be described 'on paper', so the dancers have a record of the moves they have made. I guess this is the basis of what choreography is about … though not being a choreographer, I can only speculate. A key issue is about utilising an unusual context to engage in mathematics. Functionally, the context is about communication and developing a structure or a routine based upon the divisors of 12. Another issue is how any student's work might be assessed, and this is developed in Chapter 11.

Mathematics in general across the curriculum

Science and mathematics share many common features. Both subjects deal with data, graphs, equations, etc. and common processes: collecting data, looking for patterns and connections, making predictions, hypothesising, seeking generality and so on. Thus in Science students carry out experiments or use the kind of information found on the side of a cereal packet, working with real data, crunching numbers and drawing graphs. The issue, however, is not that the mathematics department ought to teach students how to draw graphs before they need such skills in a science lesson, as this approach suggests a linear approach to learning. Furthermore, as discussed at the beginning of this chapter, such an approach also assumes students readily transfer such knowledge from one subject to another. The best way for students to learn to draw a graph is for them to have a specific need or context for doing so. Such contexts occur as much in science and geography lessons as they do in mathematics lessons. Similarly, when students write a chemical equation such as: $H_2SO_4 + Mg(OH)_2 = MgSO_4 + 2H_2O$, there exists a useful context for students to develop knowledge of balancing equations. Again here it is important to make such processes explicit so students see connections between the equations they meet in science and those they meet in mathematics.

In both primary and secondary schools, students learn about coordinates. This system is also used in geography lessons for writing six-figure grid references from maps. One difference is that in geography lessons students are likely to work with real maps and use real information to use and apply the coordinate system. The same is true for mathematics lessons when there may be more value in using real data arising more naturally through personal, social, health, citizenship, historic and geographic and scientific contexts.

From bar chart to pie chart

The process of turning a data set into a pie chart, however, is by no means a simple one, and for a history teacher to lose the thread of students' exploring issues from a historical perspective to learn the mechanics of constructing a pie chart would be a painful distraction. Problems occur, however, when students do not have the conceptual knowledge required to produce information in a pie chart, possibly resulting in off-the-cuff comments such as 'Don't they teach you this in maths?' Of course students are taught how to draw pie charts in mathematics lessons. However, we again return to the mismatch between what has been taught and what has been learnt and knowledge transfer.

Drawing a pie chart is one of the most common methods for displaying data used in several areas of the curriculum, and below I suggest an approach that may help.

The method I offer here is simple yet robust, and the example is based upon converting three groups of data – A, B and C – from a bar chart to a pie chart (I have chosen just three pieces of data for simplicity – there could be more).

The bar chart reads as follows:

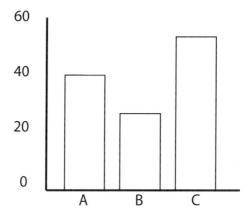

The next step is to join all three bars together into a single, complete strip. Thus, A + B + C is found, and one long strip is cut out showing the three different populations, A, B and C. Now join the ends together so the complete strip forms a circle (or a hollow cylinder).

A	B	C

The complete strip is the whole population, which now forms the circumference of the circle, and sectors can be drawn from the centre of the circle to each of the join lines between strips AB, BC and CA.

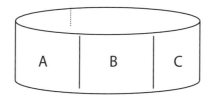

These sectors then produce a pie chart representation of the original bar chart. Although this method circumvents the need for students to carry out the calculation of dividing the combined data total into 360°, it does not lose any integrity in terms of the underlying mathematics. Indeed, such a method could provide a starting point in a mathematics lesson for students to make greater sense of the process involved in drawing a pie chart.

Helping students see connections between what they do in mathematics lessons and the contexts of other subject areas, to make explicit the implicit, is important if they are to make sense of the wider world. As such it is valuable for teachers from different disciplines to share the kind of mathematical skills they require students to use – in this way, departments can work together to create a coherent experience for students. This obviously takes time and devoting 'closure' days for teachers to work together on cross-curricular issues is essential if such sharing is to be feasible.

8

Functional mathematics

Asking 'What is functional mathematics?' is a useful place to begin to make sense of what teaching and learning functional mathematics might look like. In this chapter we consider this question and offer experiences of working within the functional mathematics agenda.

Essentially, functional mathematics is about students working within authentic contexts and recognising the purpose of mathematics arising from such contexts. Such contexts require students to use and apply existing and often intuitive knowledge to carry out a task or solve a problem.

Key processes that drive students' engagement with functional mathematics projects are:

a) Making sense of and representing mathematical information. This inevitably involves decision making about the suitability of methods, operations and tools used.

b) Analysing information by examining patterns and relationships and by changing variables within a context.

c) Interpreting the outcome of such analysis and drawing conclusions about the effectiveness or the appropriateness of the methods used.

d) Communicating a) and b) and c) to specific audiences.

Clearly, such processes can only be applied within a context, a situation or a problem to be solved. Functional mathematics-type contexts are usually related to life beyond the immediacy of a mathematics classroom, such as:

✓ environmental issues;

✓ in the home;
✓ in the workplace;
✓ in leisure time;
✓ in health and fitness;
✓ in personal finances;
✓ in life's broader issues, such as safety (e.g. Bowland maths case studies: 'How risky is life?' and 'Reducing road accidents').

Real-life contexts, and to whom do they pertain?

During a recent summer holiday Peter built a 20-metre rill to carry water from one part of his wild flower garden to another using large stones bought from an architectural reclamation yard. We mention this event because it begs the question: what mathematical skills did Peter use to complete this task? He knew he would need to use ratio to make a sand/cement mortar. However, what he didn't know at the outset was he would also construct two scalene triangles using a ruler and a pair of compasses to make templates for two triangular pieces of slate. Peter had waited the best part of 40 years before he needed to use such triangle construction skills in a real-life situation – the point being, it is often impossible to predict when and where one might use discrete mathematical skills, an issue even more complex in mathematics classrooms.

Seeking to encourage teenagers to 'buy into' their teachers' own 'real-life' contexts is problematic and great skill is required by a teacher to cause students to learn mathematics through contexts that may not be of immediate interest to them. Clearly, the issue of relevance to students is important. As such, strong motivating factors depends upon the appeal, the authenticity, the immediacy or the intrinsic value a context might offer students. Other issues are about students having choices, being able to make decisions about some aspects of the work they do and having opportunities to work with greater independence. Such issues relate closely to adolescent development per se.

A further aspect of functional mathematics is to offer students opportunities to think creatively whilst applying themselves within contexts that offer scope for problem-solving. For example, in one school I visited pupils were making key fobs that were to be sold for charitable purposes during a design and technology project. Students had to consider issues of the shape and size of their key fob as well as constructing a repeated design to decorate the fob and to consider the issue of minimising waste. There was a clear degree of motivation in the classroom. Of course, there is a strong connection between geometric constructions within mathematics classrooms and the processes students carry out in technology/design classrooms. What I observed was one small part of wider collaboration connecting these subject areas.

How do you know you don't like broccoli?

Utilising contexts students themselves are likely to be interested in or contexts through which students' interest can be stimulated is clearly important. One thing we can be fairly certain about is that our 'adult' contexts, such as working out VAT, income tax, decorating a bedroom, putting up shelves or the price of fuel, are unlikely to be contexts that will immediately arouse students' imaginations or provoke a desire for them to enquire into such issues. As such, functional mathematics projects need to be rooted in students' everyday lives, their current concerns, or possibly their future–immediate interests and concerns. Finding out what any of these interests or concerns are might be a useful starting point. Indeed, asking the students what they understand 'functional mathematics' to be can create a healthy discourse and one that offers students both ownership of and responsibility towards their learning.

However, there is also the 'broccoli' issue! This is about opening up new situations to learners. If they have never experienced something before, they will not be in a position to make a rational decision about whether it is useful or interesting – i.e. whether or not they like broccoli. There is also the issue of how a teacher presents any stimuli. Returning to broccoli, this is about how it is presented in the first instance. There is likely to be a different response to broccoli that has been boiled to broccoli that has been stir-fried with fresh ginger, garlic, some chili, a few mushrooms and a tablespoon of oyster sauce (I suddenly feel hungry) served with rice or noodles.

An interesting approach a form tutor (also a mathematics teacher) employed was to set her Year 8 tutees the task of finding out about the mathematics that related to an interest or to an event in their lives. The project was set up six weeks prior to the first student giving a presentation, usually a PowerPoint, to the rest of the class. Some examples students worked on were based upon:

- ✓ The mathematics on my journey from home to school;
- ✓ The shapes around me;
- ✓ The measures I use by comparison to those my grandparents used.

Each student then had the task of creating a ten-minute presentation on his or her chosen topic area and after the initial six-week period three students presented each week during form time. This obviously meant those students who presented later had more time to prepare. This was not, however, a competition, although students were clearly keen to do their best. In the intervening period up to the first presentation, the teacher offered support by talking to her students and checking they were not struggling to create their presentations and meet their deadlines.

A real, real-life project: congestion charge

During 2008 Peter was invited to participate in a Functional Mathematics project through the Qualifications and Curriculum Development Agency (QCDA). At the time the mathematics department at Peter's school was situated on the top floor of an extension to the ubiquitous 'ROSLA' (Raising of the School Leaving Age) block. There were seven mathematics classrooms and further along a narrow corridor three history classrooms. At certain times of the school day the sheer number of students using the corridor when leaving their lessons combined with those students arriving for either mathematics or history lessons resulted in serious congestion, particularly at a point just outside Peter's classroom door. Several of the older male students believed the best way to clear the congestion was not to allow time for the numbers to decrease but to 'charge' the blockage by pushing their way through. This resulted in a serious health and safety issue, particularly for the smaller Years 7 and 8 students, who were in danger of being crushed.

Peter decided this was an important issue and one that could be investigated and analysed with possible recommendations being proposed about how to reduce the risk of congestion. He decided, therefore, to give this problem to his Year 10 class to solve.

Introducing the problem was clearly not an issue, as the pupils had suffered four years of negotiating the maths corridor. However, because Peter had not carried out his own analysis, he simply gave them a copy of the school timetable and a list of all of the class sizes for every subject taught in every year and asked them to identify key times on particularly busy days when congestion would most likely occur. The final part of the task was to suggest possible and practical solutions to the problem. It was agreed that demolishing the block was a possibility, but not unfortunately a practical one.

Students worked in groups of threes and began the task with no further guidance, though Peter was obviously on hand to provide help if and when needed. It did not take long before Tuesdays were identified as the worst day, when there were ten mathematics and history lessons every hour with approximately 220–250 students leaving at the end of one lesson to be replaced by another 220–250 students. No wonder there was congestion.

So, having done a lot of data analysis to confirm where, when and why congestion occurred, the students had to seek solutions. There was one obvious solution, which was to unlock a door on the ground floor that would provide an alternative route to the three history rooms and at least one of the maths rooms. In the six years Peter had been at the school this door had always been locked, but nobody knew why. It turned out one of the school's Geography teachers (many years ago) had insisted the door was locked because students were using the entrance to go upstairs to history and mathematics instead of using the door just for Geography. No self-preservation there, then!

Students also observed some practices by teachers who simply dismissed their classes from their rooms without checking the state of the corridor, resulting in seven classes being dismissed simultaneously. The students proposed that, at key times, some classes should be dismissed a minute or two early in a carefully orchestrated procedure that required the class closest to the stairs to be dismissed first, followed by the next group in the adjacent room and so on. One of the groups modelled this situation and timed how long it would take for students to walk out of their classroom. They came up with a critical timeframe, indicating the majority of students would have left the building before the next groups started to arrive.

Each group made PowerPoint presentations of their findings and solutions. The best presentation was presented to the Senior Leadership Team and subsequently to the school governors. During the summer holidays two new external doors were added downstairs and one of the corridors was blocked off to ensure the students used the (by now) newly unlocked door by the Geography rooms. The functional mathematics work carried out by the students resulted in real-life changes in the school building and reduced the congestion on the corridors.

Bowland Mathematics

The resources supplied by the Bowland Trust provide excellent opportunities for students to demonstrate functional skills. Given these materials have been in the domain of mathematics teaching since autumn 2008, we envisage many mathematics teachers will have had some engagement with them. In brief, there are 19 case studies and 5 professional development (PD) modules. The case studies offer a wide range of contexts where pupils can solve problems and engage in mathematical thinking. The professional development modules provide departments with opportunities to consider pedagogic and resource issues that underpin the use of the case studies. Unfortunately, many departments, in our experience, tend to ignore the PD modules. This is something of a missed opportunity because these contain interesting contexts and ideas, such as organising a table-tennis tournament, a sweet packaging/design problem and building a school in Honduras from recycled plastic bottles filled with sand. The Bowland PD resources include examples of how the teacher can encourage independent problem-solving. This includes suggestions about how to turn questions students might ask the teacher back on themselves so students learn to become less teacher-at-the-font-of-all knowledge dependent. Peter always asks students to work in pairs or groups of threes when working on Bowland ideas and there are always a variety of methods used to develop solutions.

Organising a table tennis tournament

Peter has used the table-tennis tournament idea on several occasions with both Key Stage 3 and Key Stage 4 groups, culminating in a variety of different methods and techniques being used by students. A motivational factor with this piece of work is the ownership of the problem. This develops as students choose which people are participating in the tournament rather than a random set of names being given to them by the teacher. A challenge for the teacher is to resist the temptation to guide students down a particular route in order to reach a solution. Thus students are encouraged to develop their own lines of enquiry and seek their preferred solutions. In Peter's experience he often finds it is the extra detail that students include in their work that confirms they have been engaged with the task. For example, one arranged food and drink intervals into her schedule/solution within the given time parameter. Another student was concerned because there were an odd number of competitors so there was always one player sitting out. To overcome this issue, the student decided to run a raffle (in order to 'raise money') and the person with the winning ticket played games against the extra player. However irrelevant one might think such details were, Peter recognised their importance: the students were applying themselves purposefully to the wider context within which the problem arose. All too often we can disregard or dismiss students' ideas because they appear to be superfluous to the solution of a problem. Yet 'Functional skills are the practical skills in English, information and communication technology (ICT) and mathematics that allow people to work confidently, effectively and independently in life' QCDA website (accessed September 2010).

If we want students to become independent problem-solvers, to take initiative and demonstrate autonomy, then it is important to recognise students' different ways of making sense of what they are doing. This is also about students taking ownership of a task.

The sweet packaging design problem

Again, Peter has used the sweet packaging design problem with both Key Stage 3 and Key Stage 4 groups. With a Key Stage 4 group, Peter noticed one student was reluctant to start the task and couldn't see the point of everyone producing their own net. She needed the comfort of seeing that her net looked like everybody else's. Peter pointed out that the main purpose of the task was for each student or group of students to produce a unique design – the intention was not for the class to produce identical designs. Forty-five minutes later a sweet package was delivered to Peter with its own brand name, a tag line, a list of ingredients with sugar, salt and calorie content and health warnings included. The reluctant student was also a keen food technology student and saw the task as an opportunity to display her other skills. The sweet packaging problem, therefore, created a marvellous context for cross-curricular skills to be used and applied.

How risky is life?

This is about the causes of accidental death in England and Wales during 2005. Not the most cheerful of topics, but one that explores the extent to which sensational media reports often distort and influence the perceptions of the general public.

Peter's Year 9 class was working on this case study and had looked at the low levels of accidental death in England and

Wales. They were about to look at the life expectancy of males and females when there was a knock on his classroom door. In walked Ibrahim (not his real name for purposes of confidentiality), a person of African origin who understood Peter was expecting him. Well, due to a breakdown in communication, Peter wasn't expecting him, but nevertheless welcomed Ibrahim and invited him to sit at the back of his class and observe. It transpired Ibrahim was spending three weeks in the school as part of a mathematics degree he was studying, which encouraged undergraduates to consider teaching as a career.

The lesson continued and students recognised an increase in the deaths of males aged 17–21, which they attributed to an increase in road accident fatalities involving 'boy racers'. Despite this, there was a general opinion that England remained a very safe place to live. Towards the end of the lesson Ibrahim asked if he could say something about the lesson. He explained to the class that he was an asylum seeker and had fled his country because he was outspoken in his criticism of the government and had been warned he was going to be arrested and imprisoned because of his views. Ibrahim had chosen England as his destination because it had a reputation of being a fair country and was a safe place to live. Ibrahim now had 32 students and a member of staff open-jawed and wondering what the next revelation would be!

Some sections of the media tend to portray asylum seekers as scroungers living off benefits, but as Ibrahim explained, he had been forced to give up a well-paid job as a scientist, leave his wife and two young children behind and was now studying at the local university and hoping to secure a job so he could pay for his family to come to live with him in the UK. Ibrahim's final comment was that people in his country of birth did not expect to live much beyond 50–55 years of age, compared to 75–80 years in the UK. As you can imagine, Peter's lesson suddenly and dramatically took a completely different course: this was clearly a once-in-a-lifetime opportunity. However, the point is that if the class had been drawing and analysing data from a textbook rather than studying 'real data', then Ibrahim's story may never have been told, and a group of 14-year-old students would not have had such a fascinating mathematics lesson or received such amazing insights.

Peter has utilised many of the Bowland case studies and in his role as head of faculty has encouraged colleagues to work together to look at the materials and to plan how most effectively to use them with their classes. A key issue is about the vast amount of resources that Bowland has produced. Thus when staff collaborate, share their planning and their classroom experiences, everyone benefits. As with any curriculum development initiative, once an idea or a resource has been used for the first time and evaluated, teachers have this idea for life.

The Achievement in Mathematics (AIM) project

The AIM project was funded by the philanthropic arm of the GE Foundation and supported by the NCETM (The National Centre for Excellence in the Teaching of Mathematics). The project was aimed at improving young people's basic mathematics skills, and making them aware of work-related contexts through which mathematics is used and applied. All of the outcomes of the project appear on the NCETM portal and can be accessed via https://www.ncetm.org.uk/resources/9085.

My involvement in AIM was to work with colleagues from the Leeds area to construct and pilot resources for classrooms that we believed fell under the banner of functional mathematics. Various resources were constructed, which included:

- ✓ Using NHS statistics
- ✓ Mathematics in the workplace
- ✓ Mobile phones and mathematics
- ✓ Analysing a weather page
- ✓ Codes and ciphers
- ✓ Smoking and health
- ✓ Tilings and polyhedra

I have not provided a précis of any of these resources, as you will be able to access them through the NCETM portal. The important issues are, firstly, knowing that such resources are available and secondly, considering how a similar approach might be constructed by teachers in their own school contexts.

Another aspect of the AIM project involved interviewing and filming some GE employees to explore what mathematics they used on a daily basis within their work. Organising and planning were clearly important, as was problem-solving. Employees also discussed the need to use and apply basic mathematical skills.

One implication for schools, on a wider front, is about filming local employees having first determined they have something pertinent to offer with the intention of using such recordings as stimuli in mathematics lessons. This, of course, would be a sizeable undertaking. However, cross-curricular work is most potent when larger projects such as this are developed by different departments within a school. So, for example, the filming and the editing might be done by a media-based department perhaps in conjunction with the English department. Of course, any such filming depends upon the goodwill of the wider general public. However, we all have friends who might be prepared to talk about how they use and apply mathematics on a daily basis. Consider, for example, the work a nurse, a mechanic or a plumber does.

At one point in the AIM project I went off into a different stratosphere and came back with the following wheeze. Supposing you were able to make such a film and, having showed it to a class, the actual person in the film should walk into the classroom, ready to take any questions. Yes, I realise this is something that would take a massive amount of organization, but just imagine the impact upon the students!

Functional mathematics and coursework ... or 'new clothes for old'

Functional mathematics-type projects have enormous potential. However, the development of functional mathematics since 2007 is a subset of what some teachers defined as coursework when it was a component of assessment at GCSE from 1986.

135

Students had to learn to write about some mathematics they had been exploring. Yet we all know about the demise of coursework: having been hijacked by examination boards, how it was turned into a meaningless routine of giving marks for carrying out relatively closed tasks. This demise was further cemented by politicians who failed to see the value of students researching mathematical problems and situations under the guise of 'cheating'.

Because coursework is no longer used as a vehicle to support learning it is even more important that the original pedagogy that supported the rise of coursework is not forgotten. Even more important is to recognise how coursework-type approaches to teaching and learning can be utilised in classrooms, in part under the heading of 'functional mathematics'. Underpinning coursework was the value of students carrying out research, making decisions, interpreting and evaluating information and communicating understanding. The following description of 'Prime Practice', taken from an Ofsted report 'Understanding the Score' (2008), is wholly in line with the pedagogy upon which coursework was based:

> *Groups of Year 6 pupils thought up ideas, consulted the rest of the school, and then planned their projects, including a healthy eating tuck shop and outdoor play. They carried out research through questionnaires, collating their findings, using ICT very well. They researched costings, knowing they were expected to prove best value by comparing prices. The pupils devised criteria to ascertain which projects went forward to the judging panel, which comprised five governors, the chair of the Friends of the School and the headteacher. For this, they created presentations that gave a rationale, statistical analysis and justification for their project, including graphs and charts for visual impact, to convince the panel to part with their money.*

The context for the work these pupils carried out was realistic, purposeful and functional. The situation was 'real' to the pupils' lives and the processes they engaged with clearly had both purpose and function.

If such classroom practices are to be valued and are to become a natural aspect of the teaching of mathematics throughout primary and secondary schools then someone at government level is going to have to realise that seeking to assess the skills required for students to work in such way cannot be reduced to them answering simplistic, unrealistic test questions while sitting still in a room, usually on a hot summer's day!

9

Mathematics and ICT

Prior to becoming a teacher Peter studied Computational Science for his degree and spent 12 years in industry writing computer software. He is, therefore, a competent user of ICT, including an Interactive White Board (IWB), which he describes briefly below.

Though I am fortunate that my background gives me the confidence to work with ICT in mathematics classrooms, it is also important to recognise how many of today's students have no fear of computers. This is because they have no experience of life before computers, so it is important to appreciate how students in our classes have grown up with laptops, mobile phones, iPods, etc. For example, a 14-year-old nephew can connect all manner of electronic equipment to the television without thinking of reading the instruction manual. As such, we may sometimes need to allow ourselves to be a learner. I remember using a PowerPoint presentation with a class and wanting to start part way through the slides. I began at the first slide and quickly clicked through to another slide at which point a rather bemused student told me all I needed to do was to click a particular icon and I could start wherever I wanted. After the initial embarrassment of not knowing this I thanked him for teaching me something and the lesson continued.

A good case in point is Logo: all I need do is to give students some basic instructions and I find they work independently or support each other in ways adults find more difficult. I use the free downloadable version 'MSW-Logo', which has been installed across the school's network.

The main reasons I use Logo are to enable students to produce:

✓ *regular polygons, requiring students to understand and use their knowledge of external angle of a regular polygon;*
✓ *tessellations: the drawings can be saved as GIF files and opened up*

in Paint to allow quick colouring, copying and pasting to produce colourful display work;
✓ tiling designs that require the application of Pythagoras' Theorem and the tangent ratio. Once again, these can be copied and manipulated in Paint to emphasise the effectiveness of the computer as a tool;
✓ reflections of shapes to highlight how lengths are unchanged but the directions are all reversed, i.e. left turns become right turns and vice-versa;
✓ enlargement of shapes that highlight how angles are unchanged but lengths are scaled;
✓ rotations of shapes to create new designs with different orders of rotational symmetry;
✓ their own procedures, and this highlights the use of algebra by assigning variables that require numerical inputs.

For example, the procedure

To poly :n
Repeat :n [fd 100 rt 360 / :n]
End

This uses the number after 'poly' to draw a specific number of side, e.g. poly 5 draws a regular pentagon of side 100. The key learning here is based upon students making sense of why the procedure works and what, geometrically, the instruction 360 / :n means.

I strongly concur with all these approaches. A further strategy I have made good use of is called the 'mantle of the expert'. This strategy, adapted from the work of Dorothy Heathcote, involves working with half a dozen volunteer students prior to a specific lesson. This entails giving them enough input, say over a lunch break, so they have enough information to teach two of their peers how a piece of software works or what instructions are required to produce certain outcomes. Some examples, including the use of Logo, are i) creating sequences using a spreadsheet, ii) programming a graphical calculator, iii) using menus with function/graph plotting software. The power of this strategy means I have several 'teachers' in the room and do not therefore have to provide a full class with specific procedures, which can at times be problematic.

Peter uses various other software packages with students. However, he has often met with difficulties of accessibility and reliability: accessibility to the ICT room, plus the reliability of the computers and the school's network. He describes such difficulties below.

A central issue is the accessibility of ICT in the mathematics classroom. I have been fortunate to work in a school where the mathematics department had 16 laptop computers stored in a transportable recharging unit so staff had reasonably good access. In contrast, the remaining schools I have worked in all had dedicated ICT rooms where discrete ICT lessons were taught and all other teachers had to book these rooms sometimes several weeks in advance. This lack of availability of computers creates a situation where the use of ICT in mathematics becomes a 'one-off' or a series of lessons. This militates against students being able to use ICT as a resource to solve problems when the need arises. For example, developing an algebraic expression for interior and exterior angles of regular polygons can be done effectively without using ICT. However, if students can subsequently create a spreadsheet to check their algebra, they need immediate access to a computer. Without such access they are unable to connect algebraic thinking with the procedural thinking involved in writing a spreadsheet.

In another recent lesson, I posed the problem of calculating the perimeter of regular cyclic polygons drawn using a circle of radius 0.5m. Students had previously learnt how to use trigonometry to find lengths and angles in right-angled triangles. We began with an equilateral triangle and this required the students to create right-angled triangles by drawing radii and lines of symmetry on their diagrams. Once they had successfully calculated the perimeter of the equilateral triangle, they repeated the procedure to calculate perimeters of other polygons. Clearly, the size of the angles and the number of sides varied depending on the polygon, but the procedure for finding the perimeter was the same. Whilst planning this lesson I created a spreadsheet that calculated the perimeter of any polygon. The spreadsheet also highlighted how the perimeters of the polygons increased as the number of sides increased, each time getting closer to pi. Highlighting the columns containing the number of sides and their perimeter in the spreadsheet allowed me to generate a graph, which gives a visual demonstration of the perimeters getting closer and closer to 3.14159 …

In a subsequent lesson I showed the spreadsheet to my class. They were all familiar with using spreadsheets having been introduced to them in their ICT lessons, but they had never been given a scenario or problem like the one I had posed. If the link between spreadsheets and mathematics and the role of the spreadsheet as a powerful problem-solving tool is not made by students then ICT lessons and mathematics lessons can remain discrete, disconnected events.

Interactive White Boards (IWBs)

Though I have used IWBs intermittently since 2000, I have never taken full advantage of the potential an IWB can offer as a teaching and learning tool. However, Peter's experiences with IWBs are somewhat more progressive, as he explains below.

IWBs became available in schools at the turn of the century, though they had been used in industry for many years prior to this. I was fortunate enough to win a BBC Technology in Schools competition where the first prize was an IWB, my school being the beneficiary. The school wished to make it available to all teachers so installed it in a classroom that could be booked by members of staff. Unfortunately, with regard to ICT development, history repeated itself, and after the first term no one had used it, the reasons being lack of time, fear of ICT, lack of interest, the expense of sending staff on training courses, etc. Subsequently, I was re-timetabled to teach all my lessons in said IWB room! This was fantastic, as it gave me full access to this new teaching aid: all I had to do was to find out how to operate it using the training manual. Eleven years on, and I cannot imagine what it would be like not to have access to an IWB in my classroom. Here is a list of the advantages of using an IWB:

1) I can create professional-looking teaching resources that focus students' attention.
2) Resources are paper-free, so can be used time and again with no extra cost.

3) I can draw perfect pentagons, parallelograms, circles, etc. using the tip of a finger.

4) I have access to the internet and hence a vast set of resources: the 'Pi Song' is a particular favourite of mine. Unfortunately, sites like YouTube are often banned by network managers, and so fantastic clips of 'Juggling in a Cone' can no longer be viewed by a whole class.

5) I can project to the class a sheet from a spreadsheet, a graph, the output from a Logo program, diagrams from geometry software, etc.

6) Everyone can see it, so it is far easier to demonstrate how particular pieces of software can be used.

7) Students are keen to use the IWB to demonstrate to their peers something they have understood or achieved.

8) A record of the maths lesson as it evolves is stored on the computer.

9) I can look back at events that happened 5 minutes, 55 minutes or 5 days ago. For example, I still have a file on my laptop called 'Cheryl's lesson', which I saved after a student, Cheryl, took over the role of the teacher and demonstrated how to calculate the lowest common multiple of numbers using the product of prime factors. Whenever I subsequently teach this module of work I can always choose to show students Cheryl's work, assuming nobody from the current class pre-empts a need for me to do so.

10) Students can prepare their own PowerPoint presentations and share them with the rest of the group.

11) The pen doesn't run out of ink!

Of course, it can take many hours to prepare files for use on the IWB, and I need to be prepared to put the effort in to build up resources.

At more advanced technological levels, the IWB can be used in conjunction with:

1) a visualiser to project examples of students' work from their books for the whole class to see;

2) students, who can write on a tablet in front of them, and this appears on the board;

3) some IWBs are able to communicate with hand held devices to record students' responses, which can be stored and analysed.

'Less advantageous' uses of IWBs

I cannot see any disadvantages of using an IWB. However, I have heard of them being used and have used them used myself in ways I suspect do not support learning as effectively as they might. Some examples are:

The use of commercial PowerPoint presentations

These are available to teach any maths topic you can imagine. I know of one school that banned the use of this piece of software because every maths lesson was a series of pages from a PowerPoint that the teacher read out to the class! Once again the question of 'Who controls our teaching?' comes to the fore.

How interactive are students being?

I need to consider just how 'interactive' the IWB is from the students' perspective, recognising I need to find more opportunities for students to be the interactors.

Maintaining an IWB

As IWBs start to age they become less reliable. Some boards form blind spots that you can't write on. Pens become worn down and handwriting deteriorates. This, in turn, means students are less motivated to use the IWB.

Over-dependence on an IWB

I have taught in a classroom where the cable that made the IWB interactive was faulty. My lesson plan was thrown into disarray and I quickly had to rethink how I was going to teach the lesson without being able to write on the board. The technology, therefore, needs to be reliable and robust.

Having used IWBs for over 10 years, I find it hard to imagine teaching without one. They are a fantastic teaching aid and I only wish I had more time to prepare and share resources. Today's students expect to see technology being used in the classroom and with the development of smaller and faster technologies teachers will constantly be playing 'catch-up' with the next generation of students.

On a scale of Luddite to 10, I would put myself somewhat closer to the Luddite end. I offer this self-deprecation despite having bought a class set of Casio graphical calculators in 1986 and used them extensively across the 11–16 age range. I also made good use of Cabri Géomètre, different function graph plotters and Logo. However, irrespective of how clued up any teacher is about the use of ICT, is it important to consider how any piece of software is supporting effective learning.

I group software by two classifications. One is software that enables students to explore ideas, to make sense of concepts and take control of how to use it. Enabling students to use it as a resource, when they choose to, to make decisions about how to proceed with a task are ways in which learning can be supported. Under this classification I place software environments such as dynamic geometry, spreadsheets, Logo, function graph-plotting programs and graphic calculators. I also place all the software produced by the ATM in the 'enabling exploration' and 'supporting sense-making' category. Such resources offer students excellent opportunities to develop mathematical thinking and explore ideas in greater depth than they would were such resources not available. My second classification is software that is pre-programmed, where students answer questions either correctly or incorrectly. Such software is electronic versions of textbooks that contain repetitive exercises designed to keep students occupied by practising narrow skills. At worst, students are behaving similarly to Pavlov's salivating dogs. They get the right answer and are subsequently rewarded. They get the wrong answer and the reward is withdrawn.

I believe there are two key questions to engage with, which are: how does ICT help students learn mathematics; and how does ICT help teachers teach mathematics?

How does ICT help students learn mathematics?

Like any other resource, ICT is only as good as the context within which it is used. This depends upon the types of problems students are given to solve, the access they have to ICT and the way they use it. Just as a geoboard or Cuisenaire rods are not imbued with powers that offer the user mathematical enlightenment, neither are ICT resources. How any resource is used influences the learning achieved. From a learning perspective there seem to be three central issues to consider, and these are:

1 developing knowledge of different types of ICT software;
2 recognizing when it would be valuable to use an ICT resource;
3 having access to ICT at the point of need.

As Peter has already commented, current generations of students seems to hold no fear of learning how to use a new piece of software or hardware. The way students develop knowledge of how to use any ICT resource is therefore something of a mystery. More generally, there is the issue of whether we first learn how to use something and then transfer this knowledge to solve a problem, or whether we learn how to use something as a consequence of solving a problem. There is a strong case to suggest that need and context provide powerful motivators for learning. Just how much teaching anyone needs to get started with a piece of software will vary from person to person. As teacher, I must consider how much I need to offer any student to help him or her take control of the software. To recognise the value of using ICT, students must have knowledge of its existence and the confidence to apply it to the problem they are working on.

How does ICT help teachers teach mathematics?

Seeking to offer students choice in their learning inevitably means finding problems that encourage students to make decisions about how to proceed and what approaches and resources they might use in order to work towards a solution. As previously discussed, this does depend upon accessibility of ICT resources, particularly if we are to facilitate spontaneity; to help students work on the immediacy of a creative thought. These issues were aptly brought to fruition in a lesson I taught with a Year 9 class in 2010. I had posed the well-known 'Max Box' problem and within no time at many students got out their laptops and began to collect data in a spreadsheet and draw resulting graphs. Interestingly, the class teacher was concerned that because he had not 'taught' cubic functions to the class, they would struggle with the task. This proved not to be the case and by the end of the lesson, which lasted two hours, students were changing variables and well on the way to creating a general solution. There was one 'flash point' early in the lesson where one student decided to Google 'Max Box' in order to reach the general solution. This, of course, meant he would have missed out on all the important mathematical processes involved in the problem had I chosen not to intervene. In this single lesson, therefore, many issues arose, not least of all the positive use and the misuse of ICT.

10

Planning a scheme of work on pedagogic foundations

In this chapter I consider issues of planning a scheme of work and five principles upon which a scheme might be constructed. These are:

1 Creating a modular structure;
2 Using problem-posing and problem-solving approaches;
3 Making tasks accessible and extendible;
4 Providing students with opportunities to practise and consolidate knowledge and skills;
5 Recognising the pleasure of learning.

I also consider the practicalities of building a scheme of work based upon all-encompassing pedagogic principles such as encouraging fascination, creativity, etc.

Creating a modular structure

I define a module as a collection of ideas and tasks connected by a common theme or broad concept (e.g. volume, area, trigonometry, functions and so on). For students to access concepts and structures in depth they need time to learn, develop and construct their understanding of mathematics. One way to support this is to create modules based upon ideas that run for a minimum of two weeks.

Because mathematics is essentially a collection of ideas used to describe the world and a set of tools for solving problems, students need to experience mathematics in problem-solving ways. Modules, therefore, need to be based upon posing problems, exploring ideas and using and applying mathematics.

Access and extension

This is a recurrent theme in this book. To include all students and create opportunities to learn mathematics, it is necessary to offer accessible starting points so everyone can make a start. Consequently, students who have different aptitudes and potentials need opportunities to develop and deepen knowledge and thinking. Planning extension tasks for each idea within a module is essential. Of course, some extension ideas can be created by students themselves. When this happens we can be confident such students are becoming more independent learners.

An underpinning issue about teacher-suggested extension tasks relates to lesson-by-lesson planning and the questions and prompts a teacher might offer to different students. This, however, is not intended to support an exclusive or elitist approach to teaching: it is recognising some students need to spend longer practising certain skills and others need further challenges. Determining which students may benefit from further practise or new challenges is all part of the moment-by-moment decision making that occurs in classrooms.

Providing opportunities to practise and consolidate knowledge and skills

Within each module students need opportunities to practise skills that emerge naturally within the context of the problems being worked on. In this way, students see the relevance of practice. For example, when students use the square root key, say within a module based upon Pythagoras' Theorem, there are in-context opportunities to practise the skill of rounding up answers to a given number of decimal places or a given degree of accuracy.

Similarly, when students explore the impact of changing variables *a, b, c* in y = *a*x² + *b*x + *c,* they also practise the skill of sketching quadratics. Again, this occurs in a problem-solving context. A key issue is the difference between practising skills within a problem-solving context by comparison to students working through an exercise from a textbook or a worksheet.

Recognising the pleasure of learning

One of the strongest emotions that drives us is pleasure (I believe love is the strongest and fear follows closely behind). In order to help students understand mathematics they need to experience the pleasure involved in making sense of concepts; to gain the pleasure of knowing how and why something works. Over the years I have seen posters in classrooms proclaiming 'Mathematics is fun.' I am left wondering what this means and whether such fun is truly experienced by students as they engage with mathematics. Assuming notions of 'fun' and 'enjoyment' are synonymous, then the following quote from 'Mathematics: Understanding the Score' would seem important:

> *In the outstanding lessons, the teachers had high expectations of pupils' enjoyment and achievement. They made conscious efforts to foster a spirit of enquiry, developing pupils' reasoning skills through approaches that saw problem-solving and investigation as integral to learning mathematics. Ofsted (2008, 12)*

The quote clearly connects together several key issues about teaching and learning mathematics, i.e. enjoyment, achievement, enquiry and problem-solving. As such, seeking to develop schemes of work and teaching methodologies that embrace these issues is important.

Constructing a scheme of work: pedagogy and practicalities

To teach in ways that encourage problem-solving, a fascination with mathematics, imagination, initiative and flexibility of mind, within the existing climate of narrow testing may require several leaps of faith. Such ways of teaching require mathematics teachers to consider the kinds of approaches, strategies, problems, resources and methods of assessment they incorporate into teaching. For the remainder of this chapter I consider how a scheme of work might be constructed to embrace such aims while taking into account external demands.

I offer two examples of modules, each intended to develop a central concept. The first is 'Transformations' and is written with 12- to 13-year-old students in mind. The second is 'Area and Perimeter' and is written for 14- to 15-year-old students. Both examples are built upon the five principles outlined above and a structure based upon teacher expectations arising from the following three questions:

1 What knowledge do I expect students to possess and how might I find this out?
2 What, as a minimum, do I want all students to experience and understand from the module?
3 What extension tasks can I plan to deepen different students' knowledge?

Transformations module

I would expect 12–13-year-old students to have previously worked on reflections and rotations, coordinates, enlargements and possibly translations. I cannot, of course, expect them all either to have gained the same degree of knowledge and understanding or to have no understanding at all: no one begins from zero knowledge and everyone has something to contribute.

Determining what anyone knows is always a tricky business, which is why developing strategies to find out what students know, or partially know, are important. I may start the module by asking students to write a few sentences to explain what they already know and understand about something. I am particularly interested at this point in what key vocabulary students offer. Alternatively, I could give them a short diagnostic exercise. For example, I could ask students to provide answers to questions such as:

1 Explain with words and diagrams what you understand by the words 'reflection', 'rotation' and 'enlargement'.
2 What is the difference between drawing lines of symmetries of a shape and reflecting a shape in a mirror line?
3 Draw two four-sided shapes, one with no lines of symmetry and another with only one line of symmetry.

Such questions could be posed the lesson prior to starting the module and this will give me some clues for my planning and knowing where to start the following lesson.

Alternatively, I could set up a situation at the beginning of the first lesson where I invite individuals to come to the board and write odd words and phrases so we jointly construct a spider diagram as a basis for discussion. Another strategy could be to ask students to work together in pairs, to discuss and make notes on what they understand about a concept. After a few minutes I can ask different pairs to share something they have discussed with the rest of the class. All these strategies are not just intended to help me gain a picture of the knowledge certain individuals already have – they are also scene-setting strategies intended to bring to the surface the central ideas we are about to work on.

Whatever knowledge I ascertain about students' understanding, I am certainly going to pose a problem to cause them to work within the intended domain – in this instance, transformations.

One idea is for students to produce reflections and rotations (therefore initially excluding translations and enlargements) of a shape drawn on a square grid by playing around with coordinates of points that define the corners of a shape. I have come to use the phrase 'playing around with' a great deal in the last few years, essentially because that is exactly the quality I want learners to bring to their explorations of mathematical structures. To cause students to engage with transformations by playing around with coordinates, I suggest the following:

✓ What happens to a shape when the x-ordinates are multiplied by -1?
✓ What happens when the y-ordinates are multiplied by -1?
✓ What happens when both ordinates are swapped over (so the initial x-ordinates become the new y-ordinates and y-ordinates become the new x-ordinates)?
✓ What happens when ...?

Students can be encouraged to make up their rules and in this way there is a strong likelihood some will naturally produce enlargements and translations. Within a culture of students frequently being encouraged to ask 'What if?'-type questions, such outcomes are quite feasible.

A development is to consider combinations of transformation created by carrying out a rotation followed by a reflection, etc. Some students will be capable of drawing up a two-way table to show what happens when all different pairs are combined together. At this point, Group Theory is again not a million miles away – yet I am working with 12–13-year-old students.

Enabling students to understand the difference between transformation on a grid (where the grid itself is transformed) and the isometries of shapes, where positions of lines of mirror symmetry and the centre and order of rotational symmetry of shapes are considered, is clearly important. One such problem-solving task could be to produce all the pentominoes (shapes made by joining five squares full edge to full edge). This is something students are likely to have met in their primary schools, so finding the symmetries for each one should be feasible.

Another task is to consider what shapes are made when a given shape is 'unfolded' along its edges as follows. Consider the asymmetric trapezium in the diagram below.

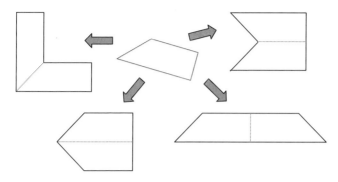

When it is unfolded four different shapes can be created: two pentagons, a hexagon and an isosceles trapezium.

By knowing the angles of the original trapezium, students can work out the angles of the shapes so formed. A further challenge is to find all the different shapes that can be made after unfolding twice. Such a problem can cause students to work systematically in order to develop initial ideas of proof in responding to a question such as: 'How do you know you have found them all?'

At this early planning stage of devising a framework of ideas I consider how, where and when ideas might fit into individual lessons so everyone can make a start on certain ideas. Deciding what, as a minimum, I intend every student to work on is an aspect of inclusion. Next, I must decide which ideas might be used as extension tasks. For example, I may choose to use a potential extension task as a starting point for everyone, particularly if I feel this will help students re-engage with concepts previously met. In this way my starter task is intended to form some kind of bridge between experiences they have had and what I want them to go on to develop. Each of the following ideas could similarly be used as starter tasks for everyone or extension work for some.

1 Asking students to find the planes and axes of symmetry of cuboids or other solids.
2 Developing the concept of enlargement so students consider what happens to the area of a shape when both integer value and fractional scale factors are used.
3 Exploring what happens when negative scale factors are applied to a shape.

155

4 Exploring what happens when a shape undergoes both a translation and an enlargement, e.g. trying to find where the new centre of enlargement moves to so two transformations can be replaced by a single enlargement: what is the new centre of enlargement after a translation of $\begin{pmatrix} 1 \\ 2 \end{pmatrix}$ and an enlargement of ×2?

I can, therefore, construct a range of ideas and tasks to plan into individual lessons. At this point of the planning process I am more concerned about what a module will look like, about how I can facilitate students' experiences of transformations. This approach matches that discussed by HMI in their 2002–2003 Ofsted subject reports (published in February 2004):

✓ In the best lessons, teachers deploy a range of teaching strategies ... to enable pupils to be more effective learners, for example to:
✓ become more autonomous and independent learners
✓ develop research and enquiry skills
✓ take more responsibility for their own progress and achievement.

Planning for students to develop such wider skills is something that needs to be applied to every module or unit of work and in every lesson.

Area and Perimeter module

The following ideas will already be used in many mathematics classrooms. What might be different is the structure of collecting a range of ideas together to form a module to run for at least two weeks. The starter task could be the context of a farmer's field and the different area of land that can be enclosed from a fixed length of fencing. My preference, however, is to set up the task using a problem-solving approach without any reference to farmers, fields or fences. This is because I question the value of expecting students to reinterpret problems by first having to situate themselves within a context that will only be real or meaningful to a small number of them. Furthermore, working on 'pure' mathematical problems is equally important as the kind of tasks described in Chapters 7 and 8. Ultimately, a scheme of work must provide learners with a range of pure and applied types of problem-solving situations.

The starting point can easily be adapted for use with a Year 6 age group, in which case I use the problem about finding all possible rectangles with an area of 24cm^2 and provide students with scissors to cut out the different rectangles drawn on 1cm^2 paper. They can then stick their rectangles on to a pair of axes, with the bottom left-hand corner of each rectangle at (0, 0). The top right-hand corner of each rectangle now lies on a smooth curve. However, for this module I consider how such a problem might be developed with a Year 10 class.

Because of the holistic nature by which different ideas are integrated into any module, a range of other skills and concepts will be drawn upon, these are:

✓ working with symbols and constructing formulae;
✓ drawing graphs (and, therefore, working with the coordinate system);
✓ squaring and working out square roots;
✓ rounding-off and writing results to a number of decimal places;
✓ working on optimisation problems, involving maximising area and minimising perimeter.

When concepts are integrated into different topic areas and become part of what happens in mathematics classrooms, from the very first lesson in Year 7, students expect to draw upon different skills and concepts at different times in a range of contexts. This is quite different from teaching concepts in separate, fragmented and isolated ways. Connecting the different skills and concepts together is at the heart of a problem-solving approach, so students automatically use and apply mathematics.

My starting point for a Year 10 class could be the same as for a Year 7 class – drawing all the different rectangles using integer values with a constant area of 24cm². My planning however develops much further as follows:

1 For each rectangle, write the dimensions and calculate the perimeter.

2 How many different rectangles (with integer dimensions) can be drawn?

3 How can we be sure we have drawn them all?

4 What are the maximum and minimum perimeters of the rectangles so formed?

5 What are the dimensions of the rectangle with the smallest perimeter?

6 What perimeter values can be gained if non-integer dimensions are used?

7 What does the graph of length against width look like?

8 What is the equation of this graph?

9 What does the graph of perimeter against length look like?

10 What is the equation of this graph?

11 What does the length against width graph look like if a different area is chosen?

12 If we know the area of the rectangle, how can the minimum perimeter be found?

13 If we begin with a constant perimeter, what different rectangles can be formed and what area does each one have?

14 What does the graph of length against width look like now?

15 If we know the perimeter of the rectangle, what calculation will produce the maximum area?

16 How can this kind of calculation be turned into a formula?

17 What does the graph of area against length look like?

18 'Equable rectangles', this is a problem from an ATM publication *Points of Departure 3* about rectangles where P (in cm) = A (in cm²), can be utilised, e.g. a rectangle with dimensions 3cm by 6cm has a perimeter of 18cm and an area of 18cm². What other rectangles have this same property?

Students could use a spreadsheet and/or a function-graph plotter to work on some of these questions, thus making a purposeful use of ICT resources.

There are plenty of questions here to develop the thinking skills of the highest-achieving students and all the time the only shape under consideration is the rectangle. Of course, it might be appropriate to suggest further problems about exploring areas of shapes other than rectangles, and this will depend upon whether students have experience of trigonometry, circle formulae and pi. If this is not the case, such problems could be revisited when such concepts are being developed.

Ideally, I want students to work on extension tasks they create themselves: the richer the mathematical environment, the more likely students are to develop their ideas and ask questions of a situation. Given the inclination children have for asking questions, it is important that in mathematics lessons this is strongly encouraged. Advocating the use of 'What if'- and 'What if not'-type questions is something that can be incorporated into mathematics lessons as a natural aspect of teaching and learning.

Problem-solving as the basis for developing modules

Within mathematics any task or problem that contains questions such as 'Why?', 'How many ...?', 'What if ...?', 'What if not...?', 'Can you prove ...?', 'What happens when we change ...?' or 'Find some more examples of ...?' are likely to provide students with problem-solving-type challenges. The ATM publication *Questions and Prompts for Mathematical Thinking* (Watson and Mason, 1998) is an excellent source for developing such questioning strategies.

Problems do not always have to represent long and arduous toil, nor do they necessarily require students to work individually. The greater the range of problems students meet and work on, the richer their mathematical diet is going to be. This approach of posing problems based upon accessible starting points and planning a bank of further questions for students to develop can be applied to every area of the mathematics curriculum. Through problem-solving, students automatically use and apply knowledge. Through problem-solving, everything is connected.

11

Teaching, learning and assessment

Teaching, learning and assessment are inseparable events. Consider the following typical scenario, the like of which occurs many times in classrooms.

> The teacher is moving around the classroom and, for whatever reason – perhaps a comment she has overheard or a glance at the student's work – the teacher asks the student a question ...

In this brief moment the teacher must either have gathered some information or believed her question would be useful for the student to think about. Perhaps the teacher had an inclination that asking the question would cause the student to:

✓ check his work;
✓ confirm an understanding;
✓ help reveal a misconception;
✓ develop a task further.

Whichever of these reasons lay behind the teacher's question is irrelevant for the purposes of the analysis of this scenario. What is relevant is the 'fact' that:

1 the teacher asked the question in the first instance, and
2 she could only do so based upon a professional judgement that the question would somehow support the student's understanding of what he was working on.

161

Professional judgement is fundamentally what assessment is about. Teachers gather all kinds of information about their students from a wide range of situations and sources. Sometimes these judgements may be partial or not wholly accurate. Sometimes they will be spot on, thus the teacher's question perhaps helped reveal a difficulty the student was having or it may have shifted the student's thinking to a greater depth.

Over time we gather all kinds of information via conversations, observations, the answers students give to questions, the questions students ask and the work they produce. What a teacher does with all this information, how much information he or she feels is necessary to record or what can remain in the teacher's head is again all part of professionalism. Of course, what information and how much is worth recording are key issues, particularly when time is finite and, though teachers are amazingly good at the art of plate-spinning, we know there are only ever 25 hours in a day! A further issue is the transitory nature of any information we choose to record and how this information is continually past its sell-by date. Okay, I shall cut to the chase.

Record of mathematical achievement

The most important information regarding students' achievements is that which can be found in records of the work students produce. However, if most of what students produce is a series of answers to tests or questions from exercises or textbooks, then the quality of any record of their mathematical achievement will be severely limited. If, on the other hand, students have had frequent opportunities to demonstrate how they have explored mathematical systems and structures, solved a range of types of problems and communicated such endeavours in a portfolio of achievement, then much assessment information will be obvious. Of course, the teacher participates in this process by responding to ongoing, developmental work as well as to completed pieces of work. Such participation will be through verbal communication, writing analytical comments based upon students' achievements and, where appropriate, advising about how they may have developed a task.

At the 2010 British Congress of Mathematics Education conference someone in the audience asked two questions towards the end of one of the keynote addresses. I cannot remember the questions verbatim: however, the gist of them were: 'What does an art student take to the next stage of her or his education or employment to demonstrate their capability?' and 'What does a mathematics student take?' I felt these were marvellous questions because they laid bare the stark contrast between a portfolio of achievement and an examination grade. The paucity of information regarding the latter when matched against the richness of information from the former should be something that ought to offer government ministers much to dwell upon as they persevere with testing. Indeed, given the move to develop a record of achievement at degree level – 'Education records to replace degree classifications' (*The Guardian* p. 9, 11 June, 2011) – there is even greater urgency to devise such an approach to replace the antiquated and wholly inadequate school examination system.

Creating portfolios of achievement, as art students do, is a valuable approach to producing a record of mathematical achievement. To do this students need to demonstrate mathematical thinking skills and communicate mathematical prowess. Completed pieces of work can be stored in folders, which students can use to self-assess achievement and which teachers can use to make professional formative and summative judgements on achievement.

Testing as a subversion of assessment and a diminution of teachers' professionality

Assessment, as a teaching and learning tool, has little to do with externally driven testing and this is because:

✓ effective assessment occurs during lessons, when teachers and students work together via the dialogue that occurs in classrooms;

✓ the quality of any assessment is dependent upon the quality of the tasks provided for students to carry out – traditional tests are low-quality tasks;

✓ teacher assessment, when combined with students' self- and peer assessment, has the potential to create a credible and substantial amount of information that reflects students' achievements;

✓ a powerful way of gathering assessment information is via students' in-depth engagement with puzzles and problems.

Sadly, the assessment agenda has been subverted and ultimately trivialised in recent years by connected factors. These are league tables and the resulting response by some school 'managers' who require staff to provide tracking data on all students up to six times a year. Even worse (if it could it get any worse), this data is required in the form of decimalised National Curriculum levels (as if such a notion exists). There are several reasons why this approach serves to subvert effective teaching and learning, and these are:

✓ An immature understanding of how learning occurs and how such learning is evaluated and measured: learning does not occur in minute, linear step-by-step ways, where students can be assessed against decimalised National Curriculum levels.

✓ Pretending we can come up with such fine gradations that measure students' knowledge, skills and mathematical thinking capabilities is complete and utter nonsense: or, in the words of a certain tennis player, 'You cannot be serious!'

✓ Target-setting should focus on both skill and knowledge development, not 'You are currently working at level 4.6 and by the end of the half-term you should be working at level 4.8' (or whatever).

✓ Once National Curriculum decimal-level data is required, the danger is such information is gathered via internal testing. As such the emphasis shifts from what a teacher 'knows' about how students engage with classwork to how they comprehend and answer closed, uninspiring questions. Percentage scores are subsequently mapped on to a decimalised level. Professional judgements are replaced by reductionist utilitarianism. Or as my mother-in-law, who worked professionally with data, says:

People get carried away by the method itself and lose sight of the core reason for collecting data in the first instance. Such people cling on to the system itself, which does not make any sense in the first instance, rather than the raison d'être ... it's not real ... they are not bothered about 'teaching' children, it's the equivalent of 'weights and measures' ... they are worrying too much about the measurement rather than the product.

✓ Narrow target levels leads to narrow, practise and drill-type teaching and learning approaches: none of the essential processes of mathematics, e.g. pattern-spotting, seeking connections, hypothesising, generalising, etc. can be measured on a National Curriculum decimal-level scale.

✓ Creativity goes out of the window.

Do we really need to stick National Curriculum levels on to children?

It is worth considering just how much and what type of information teachers need to gather, perhaps before a deputy headteacher requests the next set of grades. Professional dialogue, which informs school managers' understanding of the value of policies, systems and structures by contrast to autocratic decision-making by senior staff, is essential. An excellent example of this occurred in an 11–18 comprehensive school I worked some 35 years ago. This was a *school*. I mention this because it was not a college or an academy, just a (fantastic) school. The initiative, which involved all staff, was called 'Patterns of Decision Making and Change' (or PODMAC). This involved a series of meetings where the intended outcome was to create an agreed structure within the school for the way future decisions needed to be taken, on what basis they needed to be taken and what impact such decisions would have upon changing curriculum and learning needs. Teaching, learning and assessment were central, therefore, to this initiative. PODMAC was the springboard for enabling everyone to feel involved; of having a voice and to be able to make contributions to key decisions that would impact upon them.

A more recent example of a school that exudes democratic decision-making and one where I had the enormous privilege of briefly working in a consultancy role is a primary school in Potters Bar called The Wroxham School. Here I learnt a great deal. The school was judged as 'Outstanding' by Ofsted (March 2009) in every category. Two sentences from the lead inspector's letter to pupils read: 'You and the staff have together created an outstanding school. I was extremely impressed with how you and the staff work together to create a school where high achievement is normal and where standards in your work are high.'

I could write a whole book about the school. However, I refer to Wroxham because the teachers provide National Curriculum-level information to children and parents on only two occasions throughout the pupils' time there. These are once at the end of Key Stage 1 and once at the end of Key Stage 2, i.e. when the school has a statutory duty to do so. All the rest of the time teachers discuss with pupils targets in terms of challenges, the skills the pupils need to develop or improve upon. These targets are not about currently being at one National Curriculum sub-level and what they need to do to gain a higher sub-level: they are about developing learning in concrete terms. For example, a target might be about becoming more confident at calculating the divisors of numbers up to 30 or developing the skill of using commas and full stops.

Those two occasions apart, teachers do not need to waste time trying to dream up decimalised National Curriculum levels ... they don't get as far as levels per se. Remember, this is judged to be an 'outstanding' school in every category. The report can be viewed at www.ofsted.gov.uk/oxedu_reports/display/(id)/106846.

Here, therefore, is an example of an outstanding school that recognises the frailties of frequently labelling children according to National Curriculum levels and the potential damage such approaches cause, where pupils chase after abstract level-driven achievements instead of developing specific, concrete skills. This surely raises questions about why National Curriculum-levelled information is required so widely and why so much time and energy is wasted on gathering such data as a near-national 'educational' obsession.

Well, if we really have to ...

Of course, for many teachers, National Curriculum levels need to be gathered. There are some senior staff out there who insist such information is provided: the issue of 'whether' is not up for debate and 'why' never sees the light of day. Therefore, re-entering into the 'real' world it is worth considering how any teacher assessment information is codified and matched against National Curriculum criteria. If testing is 'the' way a mathematics department traditionally assesses students' achievements, then I offer an alternative approach: tests written by the students themselves. The idea works as follows.

Stage 1 – the teachers reviews with the students what they have been working on for the past half-term or term. A list of topics is produced together with some of the key learning outcomes to arise.

Stage 2 – the teacher discusses with students how they might write questions they think would fairly test what they have learnt. Students then write some questions and these could be handed in at the beginning of the next lesson.

Stage 3 – the teacher collects all the questions and decides which of them would be appropriate to appear on the test paper. The teacher might change the wording for the sake of clarity and add other questions if a particular topic has not been covered.

Stage 4 – the pupils do their test.

This is a method I have used from Year 7 to undergraduates. With a Year 7 and a Year 8 class I distributed the completed test questions a week before the actual test so students had an opportunity to revise. Of course, those who did take the opportunity to do so were clearly engaging in learning; thus the test served a greater purpose than merely gathering information on the scores they achieved. Important reasons for using this approach were to cede some responsibility and ownership of assessment processes to students. Furthermore, when students write questions about what they have been learning, this simultaneously enhances understanding. Here again assessment is integrated within teaching and learning.

Gathering National Curriculum level information about students' work other than through testing

Gathering National Curriculum level information may be the most boring of tasks, though annoyingly necessary when such information is required by the powers that be. Even so, we can still treat such levelling both sensibly and, if it helps, contemptuously! For example, when I used to mark postgraduate assignments where grade-related criteria boundaries were matched against percentage scores (thus a grade C was in the 50–59 range, a grade B in the 60–69 range etc), I only ever gave scores that ended in 0, 2, 5 or 8, e.g. 55, 62 etc). In my mind I classified these as follows:

0: just deserved to be in the next grade band up or I couldn't make up my mind!
2: just inside a grade band.
5: in the middle of a grade band.
8: at the top end of a grade band.

Such an approach can easily be translated into National Curriculum levelling, though first of all we need to be conversant with National Curriculum-level criteria to be able to gauge where students are 'at'. Once we have worked with a class for a few weeks it is not difficult to recognise which National Curriculum levels students are broadly operating within. The next question we can ask might be something like: is the student just inside a level, comfortably working at that level or working at the top end of a level? What I offer here is intended as a speedy way of subverting educationally oblivious colleagues, i.e. those folk who need to 'get a life'. It is about being seen to play the game. Even though it is a silly game, it is sadly all part of the game.

In the next part of this chapter I consider the kind of approaches to teacher assessment Peter has been exploring with his colleagues in the mathematics department at his school.

Peter's experiences of developing teacher assessment

Implementing and embedding teacher assessment in the department has been a slow process. The main reason for this has been a departmental over-dependence on the use of Key Stage 3 past papers as the only assessment tool. These tests have been used to produce percentage scores for students and these percentages were mapped on to National Curriculum levels. One outcome of this test-dependency meant teachers no longer needed to use their professional judgement to assess the levels of work achieved by their students. Thus teachers' capabilities to recognise, for example, the difference between a level 5 and a level 6 in, say, algebra became redundant. Consequently skills and knowledge regarding assessment faded amongst experienced staff whereas for recently and newly qualified teachers (RQTs and NQTs) this skill had never been developed. However, the demise of Key Stage 3 tests provided all teachers with opportunities to gain ownership of the assessment of students' achievements and responsibility for applying levels using criteria written into a national framework. More significantly, teacher assessment encourages more holistic approaches where assessment builds upon knowledge of what students achieve throughout the academic year rather than single snapshots, primarily based upon testing.

Having been involved in many teacher assessment conversations with other heads of mathematics within my local authority it appeared most preferred the traditional system of testing. Perhaps this is something that appeals to the 'arithmetical brain', i.e. a student scored 62 so he or she is clearly a level 5.5!

Our departmental conversations about teacher assessment will, I am sure, be similar and familiar to many teachers. At the outset colleagues were both unsure of their ability to level students' work and what they might use as evidence. Could everyday classwork be used? Could homework be used? Could verbal comments be used? The answer to all of these has to be 'yes' providing the teacher is confident it is students' own work that is being assessed and credited. Unfortunately, many staff found this a difficult concept to come to terms with.

Constructing professional approaches to teacher assessment based upon robust in-school and between-school moderation procedures has the potential for schools to wrest responsibility for assessment away from central and local government. There are several issues at stake here, which are:

Assessment for learning

By changing marking habits and moving away from tick/kiss type responses to the work students produce, the 'assessment *for* learning' approach becomes a powerful one. It enables teachers to reduce the quantity of futile marking and increase the quality of meaningful feedback.

Having opportunities for in-school curriculum development

Teachers being able to use meeting time over the course of an academic year for in-school and between-school moderation events has implications for the way senior managers enable such decision-making. Thus departments can determine how best to use meetings. The important link between quality of assessment, quality of schemes of work and, of course, the quality of teaching is too strong to be ignored.

Testing as a flawed measure of achievement

Shifting the emphasis in schools from gathering data based upon scores from tests to data based upon teachers' professional judgements is another quality issue; i.e. the quality of the data gathered as well as the quality of the purpose for which the data is used. If we are to have a quality system of education that caters for all, then the quality of the assessment procedures are paramount. Teaching-to-the-test has had a significantly demeaning impact upon learning. Testing narrows the curriculum and undermines learning for relational understanding.

Valuing teacher assessment

Assessment is an ongoing process; indeed, through moment-by-moment interactions with individual pupils the teacher automatically makes assessments in order to ask questions, pose extension tasks or consider how to help to overcome a difficulty. The complexity, however, is enormous: how much assessment evidence can feasibly, in the time available, be recorded and how much information must remain in the teacher's head? Again, this boils down to teachers' professionality.

In order to shift assessment practices away from testing towards more holistic approaches based upon ongoing classwork is an issue Peter has been keen to develop. A starting point was to use a task he believed would enable students to demonstrate both content and process skills, as described below.

The dangers of using specific tasks versus knowing where to start

Peter's initial decision to use specific tasks against which pupils might be assessed was the result of particular development related to the school calendar. Year 10 examinations, Year 9 SATs (even though they are no longer reported) and Year 8 assessments occurred over three consecutive weeks. Thus to avoid test paper marking fatigue, Peter took the decision to use a task titled Ten straws.

Ten Straws

With ten straws we can make different 'straw-crossing diagrams' using the following rules:

a) Unless all straws are parallel, straws must cross each other.
b) No crossing point can have more than two straws passing through it.
c) Straws are placed either horizontally or vertically.

Here is an example of a 10 straw crossing diagram.

There are 21 crossings.

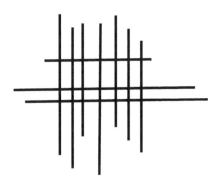

Questions:

What other number of possible crossings can be made?

The smallest number of crossings is clearly zero, but what is the next largest number of crossings? Can you explain your answer?

What is the largest number of crossings? Can you explain your answer?

Explore numbers of crossings for different numbers of straws.

Having two Year 8 classes myself, I trialled the activity with one of them, with the intention of using their work as part of a departmental CPD session.

The Year 8 students were aware that this was their 'assessment week' and wanted to know why they weren't doing tests. I explained they were going to do a different type of test, one in which they could work in pairs if they wanted to, could ask questions if they were stuck, were expected to share ideas with fellow students and there were no 'right' answers. They thought I had completely lost the plot! I planned the activity to run all week, giving students a maximum of three hours to explore the problem. The outcomes were amazing. All students except one worked hard during the three hours and there was a surprise benefit for one student who missed the first lesson due to illness: he just had to play catch-up, which was a far better alternative to being told he had missed the test and had to go and sit in the mathematics office and do it there, thereby missing another lesson!

As with all curriculum development, trialling new ideas and different ways of working are clearly important issues. Trying anything new in the classroom requires the teacher to take some degree of risk and this means stepping outside our comfort zones and seeing what else might be out there. Staying inside our comfort zones means we stick with what we know we are good at – what we don't know is what else we might be good at!

A departmental CPD session took place when some teachers were about to start the task with their classes, some were part way through and some had completed it. We were able to share our experiences and in particular discuss the significant role of the teacher in the assessment process. This initially focused on the level of support one might give to students when they are carrying out the task. For example, the skill of responding to a student's questions by asking another question is a key teaching strategy that can be applied in every mathematics classroom. We discussed that this was the same technique we had used with students carrying out the Bowland CPD tasks on the Table Tennis Tournament and the Sweet Box Design [see page 131], thus encouraging the students to make their own decisions and raising their awareness that there can be different solutions or different ways of reaching a solution to any problem.

This experience was not just about assessment because teaching, learning and assessment as discussed earlier cannot be separated into discrete boxes. Although the main focus was assessment, issues such as effective teaching strategies, using a 'new' idea and working with resources that transcend the use of a textbook are all apparent in this anecdote.

Teachers brought along examples of students' work and not surprisingly there was a vast range in the quality and quantity of the work. What was interesting was that staff commented on how well students had engaged with the task and several expressed surprise at how well certain individuals had performed. Other comments, which I have paraphrased, included:

    'This has allowed the students to show me what they know rather than a test which shows me what they don't know.'

    'I realise that many of my class always want to draw a bar chart

instead of plotting points and drawing a graph – but some of them could do it.'

'They applied previous work we had done on straight line graphs to a practical situation much better than I expected.'

'Discussions within the class resulted in many students following a particular line of enquiry and this became a real focus of their work.'

'Even the weakest students in the class were able to produce some work of their own.'

This process also helped staff to recognise different students' capabilities to use and apply mathematics. Importantly, this was an area I felt we needed to address within the department per se.

One of the complexities for mathematics teachers since the National Curriculum was introduced in 1989 has been how to incorporate opportunities for students to use and apply mathematics. Assessing students' capabilities to use and apply mathematics has, therefore, been even more complex. Within this anecdote, teachers provided students with such opportunities to use and apply mathematics, whilst at the same time engage in some algebraic thinking. This integration of using and applying within the entire mathematics curriculum is not just important – it is vital.

I also asked my classes to give feedback on the assessment process and many students had preferred the approach by contrast to a formal exami-nation. Perhaps this was because there wasn't the pressure they normally feel when doing a test. Most students preferred working in pairs and being given help when they were stuck; a few students, alternatively, said they preferred doing a test, in silence, so they could measure themselves against other students.

Discussing with students an approach to assessment that Peter used is more than just one aspect of his teaching style: it is a determined strategy aimed at providing students with opportu-nities to discuss ways in which assessment of their achievement can be done.

Overall, this was a very positive experience that has moved the whole department forward with respect to teacher assessment. Staff are now much more confident about assessing students' work and are less dependent upon using formal tests for assessment purposes.

This assessment experience can clearly be replicated and used across all teaching groups to cover the entire curriculum using a range of further tasks. Gathering together and using such tasks to assess students' achievements both formally and informally is clearly a challenge. Furthermore, the developmental process involved in embracing such a challenge has much potential with regard to professional development. Contrast if you would this approach, the degree and quality of professional development engaged in with the use of published tests as an assessment mechanism.

Finally, there is an even more substantive issue to consider, and this is exactly what 'passing' an examination in mathematics actually means, to examinees or to those people involved in students' next steps in their academic development or their employment. A report, 'Mathematical Needs: Mathematics in the Workplace', produced by an Advisory Committee on Mathematics Education (ACME) found that 'far more jobs now need mathematical problem-solving skills' ('School leavers falling behind with maths skills', *The Guardian* 14–06–11). The chair of the committee went on to suggest: 'it is not just a case of students missing out on two years of learning mathematics (post-GCSEs) … but of arriving at the next stage of their lives having forgotten much of what they did know'. I argue, however, the situation is far, far worse than students' merely forgetting what they may have previously known. We must recognise how students are taught in pressure-cooker-type examination preparation, which, as I have argued, has little to do with actually learning mathematics. This is not the purpose: the purpose is to 'pass' a test where only grades C to A* have any credibility. Thus, forgetting what they learnt in preparation for GCSE examinations is possibly a blessed relief.

Learning mathematics is about learning skills that can be used intuitively and applied to various situations. Learning anything in order to pass a test just removes all the pleasure and the value of learning in the first instance. When mathematics is learnt effectively it is akin to learning how to speak, to write, to ride a bike, to bake a cake, to play an instrument ... not merely to pass a test.

12

Developing students' thinking skills

One traditional view of teaching is of 'passing on' knowledge. When asked the question 'Why do you want to teach?' I have heard many prospective teachers respond: 'Because I want to pass on my knowledge.' This may appear a perfectly reasonable thing to want to do – after all, we have had someone else's knowledge passed on to us. It does, however, raise two issues. The first is whether one's knowledge is worth passing on. If all each generation ever learnt was knowledge passed on by a previous generation then we would find ourselves in an ever-decreasing knowledge spiral. Of course, the complete opposite happens: the knowledge base across the planet has increased at what appears to be an amazing rate. The second issue is that if future generations are going to learn more than the current generation can possibly know, what roles do teachers play in this process? What part do mathematics teachers play in facilitating the possibility of and creating the conditions for some students to go well beyond their teachers' mathematical knowledge base?

Helping students develop thinking skills in mathematics classrooms

I do not believe I can 'teach' another person to think. This is because I do not have sufficient knowledge of neurology, of how the brain works. I can, however, construct environments where students have opportunities to deepen and sharpen their thinking skills; where they can engage with puzzles and problems, simple games and even 'magic' tricks. Before going any further it will be useful to define what thinking skills are and how they connect with mathematics.

So, what are thinking skills?

In relation to mathematics, thinking skills are, in part, the process skills such as simplifying, systematising, classifying, conjecturing, predicting, generalising, proving and so on. However, knowing what thinking skills are only makes sense when there are puzzles and problems to be solved so these skills are used and applied as a matter of course. Developing awareness is crucial. I am reminded of a quotation by Gattegno, 'Only awareness is educable,' which was developed in an article by Mason:

> *Only my awareness is educable, in the sense that my power to notice can be developed and refined, and my noticing can be focused and directed. Only when I notice spontaneously, for myself, can I choose. Only when I notice my self, do I become awake and free. (1987, 30)*

Developing one's own awareness is complex: developing another person's is even more so. At best, we can cause students to reflect not just upon what they have learnt but to also upon how they achieved certain outcomes, understandings and solutions.

With this in mind it is wholly inappropriate to plan a scheme of work where thinking skills are dealt with in isolation. For example, having separate 'thinking skills' lessons suggests thinking in other lessons is not the central intention! Therefore, to enhance students' learning, thinking skills need to be integrated within and developed throughout every mathematics lesson. Encouraging students to think deeply about something, to consider alternatives, to view something from another person's perspective, to ask 'What if?'- and 'Why?'-type questions are at the root of social, emotional and rational development.

The remainder of this chapter is set out in three sections:

✓ making sense of conventions and unravelling vocabulary;

✓ exploring systems and structures;
✓ classifying, grouping, ordering and naming.

Making sense of conventions and unravelling vocabulary

One of the questions young children often ask and frequently turn into a repetitive questioning game is 'Why?' Once a child has hooked an adult into playing the 'Why, why, why?' game, there is obviously a lot of fun to be had. Asking 'Why'-type questions is probably the most potent way of trying to make sense of mathematics per se. Students need to be encouraged to go deeper into a problem and not be satisfied with only getting the 'right answer'. Enculturating students to recognise the power of knowing how and why something works, such as the 'long division' algorithm, is an important part of shifting away from the current: 'Is it going to be on the test?'-type culture. Making sense of mathematics involves knowing the conventions associated with concepts and understanding the vocabulary used to describe and to discuss mathematics. Vocabulary and symbols are gateways to making sense of mathematics. If we cannot understand the vocabulary or if the symbols are meaningless hieroglyphics, then mathematics is likely to become inaccessible and obscure. When learners understand why something works and have access to the associated vocabulary, when they make sense of what is going on, when they are included, they become more effective learners. This in turn increases motivation and self-esteem, leading to better-behaved classes … everything is connected.

Exploring systems and structures

Knowing how a system works and what happens when conditions are altered or when parameters are changed, by applying some kind of rule, underpins understanding. For example, understanding the place value system requires learners to know what happens when amounts become 10, 100 etc. times bigger or smaller. Going further to the right of the units column opens up a whole new world of numbers. Seeing columns or place value holders in terms of powers of 10 is a deeper, more complex way of describing the system.

Indeed, the place value system underpins much understanding, and there are interesting problems whose solutions only make sense if place value is brought to bear when working on a problem. A good example is as follows:

✓ Write any three different digits.
✓ Make all the possible two-digit number using combinations of these three digits
✓ Add these (six) two-digit numbers together
✓ Divide your answer by 22
✓ Write down your answer.
✓ Now go back to the original three digits you wrote down at the start.
✓ Add these three digits together.
✓ What do you notice?
✓ Why does it happen?

Extending this puzzle, we can consider starting with four digits and making either all the three-digit or all the two-digit or even all the three- and two-digit values together. Determining what value to divide the total by each time in order for the puzzles to work is the crux issue. To make sense of the outcomes place value must be taken into account.

Classifying, grouping, ordering and naming

To classify something we need to see what similarities and differences exist between objects under consideration. Classifying is essentially a sorting exercise based upon certain properties. Geometry provides many contexts for students to develop ideas of classifying, grouping, ordering and naming.

A sequence of lessons I have used on several occasions is based upon classifying shapes using Geo-strips. These are coloured plastic strips with small holes that can be joined together with split-pins. The first lesson takes some organising: however, I always found the quality of discussion that ensues is worth the extra effort required in setting up the task.

In small groups I provide students with nine strips: three long strips (**L**), three middle-length strips (**M**) and three short strips (**S**). Each group is given different lengths of strips. This is because I want groups to make different numbers of triangles from the collection of strips with which they are provided. Students are asked to make as many different triangles as possible, each time using just three strips and clipping them together by the holes at each end. I ask them to code each triangle using combinations of the symbols **L**, **M** and **S**. Some groups will be able to make the maximum of 10 possible triangles with the following codes: **LLL, MMM, SSS, LLM, LLS, MML, MMS, SSL, SSM** and **LMS**. Other groups will only be able to make a subset of these 10 triangles, and this will depend upon the relative lengths of **L**, **M** and **S**. So if the lengths of **S** + **M** ≤ **L**, or if 2**M** ≤ **L**, or if 2**S** ≤ **M**, shorter lists are only possible.

The intention is to engage students with the condition for making triangles according to the lengths of the sides by entering into a discussion about why some groups have been able to make 10 triangles whereas others have made fewer.

Using combinations of three strips is a starting point for a much more complex exploration of what happens when we use four strips to make quadrilaterals. Because of the loss of rigid structure when using just three strips the possibility of making an infinite number of quadrilaterals using four strips emerges. This forces students to organise and classify information.

The next stage is to consider how parameters affect the ways quadrilaterals can be classified. What follows will certainly appear to be a staged set of instructions and may appear to run counter to the notion of students developing thinking skills. However, my intention here is to offer a structure within which many sub-questions can be asked and students can develop their understanding of classifying at different rates according to how far they are able to develop the ideas offered.

Once some quadrilaterals have been made and the issue of an infinite number of shapes has been established, the notion of classifying according to properties can be discussed. One approach is to ask students to discuss the properties of parallel sides (Pops) and the number of right angles (RAs) that quadrilaterals can possibly have. The idea develops by students finding quadrilaterals with pairs of properties formed from 0, 1 or 2 Pops combined with 0, 1, 2 or 4 RAs. As it happens, from these twelve pairs of combinations only seven essentially different quadrilaterals can be formed. These are:

Pops	RAs	*Possible* quadrilateral
0	0	An asymmetric quadrilateral and/or a kite
0	1	An asymmetric quadrilateral and/or a kite
0	2	A kite
1	0	An isosceles and/or an asymmetric trapezium
1	2	An asymmetric trapezium
2	0	A parallelogram
2	4	A rectangle

The next and most complex aspect of this sequence of ideas is to introduce a third property: the number of equal sides (ES) any shape can have. There are five such possibilities: shapes with 0, 2, 3, 4 or two pairs of equal sides. By combining these 5 possibilities with the 7 from the table above, there are 35 pairs – the challenge is to find which of these 35 combinations of properties produce quadrilaterals.

Of these 35 possibilities only a certain number of combinations are possible. For example, shapes with two pairs of parallels and four right angles can only either have four equal sides (a square) or two pairs of equal sides (an oblong). Working systematically through all 35 combinations could form a very useful group task.

Throughout this sequence of tasks students work with properties of shapes and name and classify them accordingly. There will be much scope to discuss the vocabulary associated with quadrilaterals and consider why a square is a rectangle and what is different about an oblong; similarly a rhombus and a parallelogram. Students can also use drawing implements and dynamic geometry software to create shapes.

Because the task is accessible and equipment-rich, all students will have opportunities to develop their mathematical thinking, irrespective of their so-called level of attainment.

Integrating thinking skills into mainstream mathematics lessons

Since the Cockcroft Report in 1982 and the advent of coursework in mainstream mathematics classrooms through GCSE from 1986 there has been a growth in students 'doing investigations'. These have been characterised through problems such as Frogs, Max Box and a plethora of other investigations, many of which ended up with certain sequences of numbers, typically 1, 3, 6, 10, 15 ... and 1, 2, 3, 5, 8, 13 ... Such problems are frequently a bolt-on type of experience where students are guided towards producing and generalising sequences. Because such problems become the vehicle for assessment of coursework, GCSE students were often taught the rules of the game, which were:

✓ simplify the problem;
✓ collect results;
✓ put them into a table;
✓ write about any patterns noticed;
✓ produce a formula or general result.

This became an algorithmic process and, through the institution-alisation of investigation work, problem-solving was subjugated to the necessity of passing a test. As such, this approach bore little resemblance to the reality of trying to solve a problem where stuckness and messiness emerge. Offering problems so students have to think about something in depth, to make decisions about how to proceed, to consider what parameters might be changed, to explore different avenues and not to feel downhearted if they are unable to find a complete solution creates a more realistic view of learning mathematics.

Because such an abomination of learning occurred it was with sad relief that 'coursework', as it had become defined, was removed from the assessment lexicon. However, this was also a case of throwing out the baby with the bathwater, as rich assessment opportunities that existed before examination boards demeaned the notion of coursework were also lost. Yet, just because it is impossible to assess students' thinking skills through a timed, written test, this does not mean that putting energy into developing such skills is futile. Integrating thinking skills into the mainstream mathematics curriculum is even more important and students need to be offered a wide range of problem-solving opportunities from year dot.

In secondary education I advocate puzzling and problem-solving tasks should be used from lesson one so students gain a sense of what learning mathematics in their new school is about and thinking skills become a natural feature of lessons. Problems need to provide opportunities for students to manipulate parameters, order information, discuss different solutions and, wherever possible, prove something. For example:

> How many ways can the number 5 be partitioned by addition? This could be developed by looking at partitions of other numbers and, in turn, lead to an exploration of Pascal's Triangle (if, for example, 1 + 1 + 3 and 1 + 3 + 1, etc. are counted as different partitions).

> Using the digits 1, 2, 3 and 4 and one multiplication sign, what are the minimum and maximum products? (For example, 12 × 34, 231 × 4, etc.) This can lead to students producing systematic lists to find all possible answers.

> On square grid paper draw some shapes that have, say, five dots on the perimeter and two dots inside. What are the areas of the shapes? What happens to area as the number of dots on the perimeter and inside the shape changes?

How many different rectangles can be made with an area of 20 square units?

This could lead to work on pairs of factors and be developed into work on fractions and decimals (for example, 2½ by 8, 3.2 by 6.25). Square roots are not far away (e.g. finding the length of a square with area 20), and, because $20 = 2^2 + 4^2$, then Pythagoras could also be on the cards.

What does the graph of multiples of 2 look like? This could lead to work on graphing and comparing other sets of multiples, including multiples of a ½. What about a graph of one more than the multiples of 2 or two less than the multiples of 3?

What is the median height of the class? This could lead to finding and comparing the median heights of other classes, perhaps to calculate what the average percentage height increase is across each year group.

The pleasure of teaching mathematics in ways that cause learners to use and develop thinking skills while working on content skills is grounded in a holistic vision of learning and a heuristic view of mathematics. There are oodles of opportunities to take the simplest of tasks and extend them into more complex areas. Finding ways of extending simple, rich starting points so students can work on different levels of complexity and ultimately become capable of going beyond producing quick answers to closed questions is not just interesting and good fun: it is absolutely essential.

13

Teaching mathematics without a textbook

Call it vandalism, but those old textbooks had it coming and were destined for the bin anyway. I had been teaching for just a few weeks in my new role as Head of Mathematics and had set myself a target of seeing how long I could sustain teaching without using a textbook. I had arrived from my previous school with a lot of experience of teaching mathematics using investigative approaches. I intuitively and explicitly believed problem-solving was the most interesting and valuable way for children to learn mathematics and I wanted to develop this way of working with my new colleagues.

Three weeks into the job I decided to offer a Year 9 class the Möbius band problem, an idea I am sure most mathematics teachers will have met before. Recycling old textbooks to generate the required strips of paper seemed a better option than using pristine A4 paper. Thus I began the lesson distributing some old textbooks and asked the students to turn to any page. 'Which page?' some students asked.

'Oh, I don't know … any page. What about page 19?' I responded. 'Okay, tear out the page.'

For some, this was initially a step too far, and they thought I had lost it. Eventually, everyone did what I had asked, and while students cut strips of paper from the torn-out pages of the textbooks I dispensed sellotape to each group. Some weeks later when watching *Dead Poets' Society* I thought, *Well, I did it first!*

The task was to explore what happens when the following process is carried out.

1 Put one, two and three half twists into three different strips of paper.
2 Sellotape the ends of each strip together to form Möbius bands.
3 Cut lengthways through the middle of each joined-up strip, following the curve of each band, until something happens.

A demonstration of what happens after one twist and one cut, followed by a second cut, makes for an enjoyable and intriguing start to a lesson, particularly if students are asked to predict what they think will happen before each cut is completed. An interesting result which, at the time, I had not met before was when one student ended up with one small strip and one large strip linked together after 'one' cut down the 'middle' from a band containing a half twist. Well, it is not exactly 'one' cut and not exactly down the 'middle', but if you haven't come across this solution before you may wish to explore how it's done.

So, what were the students learning? On the cognitive side they were learning about degrees of turn, about how to classify and how to record the outcomes. They were learning about the importance of recording results systematically and seeing how to make sense of what happened. They were learning how to describe the outcomes using mathematical vocabulary. They were solving a problem and making predictions.

On the affective side they were learning that mathematics can be enjoyable, of the need to be careful and patient and that they were all capable of making a start on the task. At the end of the lesson some turned themselves into kings and queens by adorning their heads with Möbius bands: given this was the last lesson of the day and their excitement would not need to be quelled by a colleague, I felt comfortable with this outcome. They were also learning that mathematics did not need to reside in the pages of a textbook or the teacher's head: active, practical tasks were to become a regular feature in their mathematics lessons.

I learnt that if I had enough 'rich' starting tasks I could provide students with access to the entire mathematics curriculum. This notion of 'rich' tasks was first conceived or defined in 1987 in a project called 'Better Mathematics: A Curriculum Development

Study' directed by Afzal Ahmed. The following list was drawn up by a group of teachers attending an in-service course. The list read:

WHAT MAKES A RICH MATHEMATICAL ACTIVITY?	
It must be accessible to everyone at the start.	It should promote discussion and communication.
It needs to allow further challenges and be extendible.	It should encourage originality/invention.
It should invite children to make decisions.	It should encourage 'what if' and 'what if not' questions.
It should involve children in speculating, hypothesis making and testing, proving or explaining, reflecting, interpreting.	It should have an element of surprise.
It should not restrict pupils from searching in other directions	It should be enjoyable.

(1987, 20)

Each of these is an aspect of pedagogy in which textbooks have no place. However, there are further reasons for not using textbooks, and these are about:

✓ Teacher autonomy;
✓ Real-life contrivances;
✓ Student ownership of learning and teachers' ownership of teaching;
✓ Strategies beyond using a textbook;
✓ Student dependence on textbooks;
✓ Practising and consolidating skills and knowledge.

Teacher autonomy (or ... Who controls my teaching?)

If one of the main purposes of a textbook is to allow students to practise a skill and consolidate knowledge, I am interested in how

I can cause students to achieve the same outcome using different strategies and approaches. One of the difficulties with textbooks is they allow authors to invade our classrooms, giving problems to children they obviously do not know and making assumptions about individual student progression that they cannot possibly make. This progression is usually set out in a chapter-by-chapter, exercise-by-exercise approach. Yet why should I relinquish responsibility for progression and structure to another person when I know nothing of the pedagogy upon which they attempt to direct and order my students' learning?

We have been controlled for too long by politicians, some local authority advisors and former strategy consultants seeking compliance from teachers. It seems crazy therefore to pay authors of textbooks to further control how we teach, especially given the cost of textbooks and how this could be spent on far more valuable resources.

Real-life contrivances

Here is another reason for not using a textbook relating to 'real-life' contexts. This is because they are out of date the moment they are bought and there is most certainly an absence of references to real, local sources. Consequently, any chapter based upon real-life information is likely to be a contrivance and largely irrelevant to our classrooms and to adolescents' lives. For example, I have seen chapters on algebra suggesting plumbers and electricians work out what they are going to charge customers according to certain formulae. Do we believe this is how most plumbers and electricians actually cost out jobs? This is clearly not the case – it is merely some pseudo excuse for teaching algebra. Students are not only being misinformed about real-life situations, but they are also being provided with disingenuous perspectives on the uses of mathematics. If we want student to really engage in real-life situations then they either need to be out there in real life or, as suggested in the chapter on functional mathematics, we need to bring real-life people into the classroom. They certainly do not want to be working from a textbook.

Students' ownership of learning and teachers' ownership of teaching

The importance of ownership is about students being able to gain greater control over what and how they learn. Questions in textbooks are mostly closed, uninteresting and inevitably rhetorical and the same page-by-page path has been trod by many students of previous generations. The implications are that uncritical use of textbooks undermines ownership, stifles creativity and provides students with unimaginative and uncreative ways of learning mathematics.

Enabling students to achieve ownership of mathematics via the ways they learn mathematics is not difficult. Essentially, we need to cause students to collect data and work with that data, not only within statistical or probabilistic situations but throughout numeric algebraic and geometric contexts. For example;

> **Find all the different consecutive sums for each of the numbers between 1 and 30.**

This problem enables data collection, which leads students to classify numbers according to different properties they have, e.g. different sets of multiples, triangular numbers, powers of 2, prime numbers, numbers in the sequence $4n + 6$, etc. all have properties connected to consecutive sums. Once students have gathered their data they can analyze it and start to look for connections. How data is gathered in the first instance will depend upon how the teacher wishes students to experience this aspect of the task; this, in turn is about the teacher's ownership of the task and where such a task might best fit within a scheme of work.

Student dependence on textbooks

I recently heard a head of mathematics complain that when he uses problem-solving approaches, instead of working from a textbook, some of his students ask: 'Is this going to be on

191

the test?' It almost seems schools are becoming consumer-led organisations where all students want are examination grades and to achieve these they do not wish to be bothered with anything that does not immediately appear to help them achieve this aim. Imagine how such consumerism is going to play out at in the brave new world of universities charging up to £9000 a year in fees.

For students, an over-dependence upon textbooks can result in them believing that mathematics is predominantly about getting right or wrong answers and success is measured by the number of ticks they receive. The dangers of students working in such ways are ubiquitous. Conversely, providing more open-ended types of situations results in students developing abilities to think something through and develop a range of ways of learning.

In the remainder of this chapter I consider strategies to support the teaching and learning of mathematics. The first focuses on ways to encourage students to develop concepts and to practise and consolidate skills.

Practising and consolidating skills and knowledge

There are hundreds of problems and situations that can be set up for students to work on to practise skills and consolidate their understanding of concepts. Such practice and consolidation arises when students repeat processes so they use skills to seek solutions to bigger problems. A simple example is when students are asked to engage with the palindromic multiplication problem. This is about multiplying two two-digit numbers together that produce the same product when the order of the numbers are reversed, i.e.

96 × 23 = 32 × 69
How many more palindromic multiplication calculations exist?

In this problem students practise the skill of multiplying two

two-digit numbers together. However, as students recognise there is something 'going on' relating to the individual numbers being divisors of another value, they also consolidate their knowledge of divisors.

Here are two further contexts I develop in greater depth. The first is based upon using a nine-pin geoboard. This is a piece of equipment made from a block of wood and nine nails arranged in a 3x3 square. The size of the board is in the region of 15 to 20cm square. Over time I have made dozens of these. Using 15mm Escutcheon pins, bright golden nails with round heads, produces a beautiful finished item.

The nine-pin geoboard, brought to mathematics teaching by Gattegno, is possibly the most remarkable piece of equipment for providing students with access to a wide range of mathematics and for providing the teacher with the potential for generating an amazing amount of ideas. It is a 'closed' environment from which many 'open' problems arise. The power of the nine-pin geoboard lies in its simplicity and the fact it can be made from scrap wood, a lick of paint, a hammer and a few nails.

Generating problems on a nine-pin geoboard

One strategy I find useful is to give out the equipment and grid paper and seemingly 'ignore' students' questions or turn strategically deaf for the next few minutes. My experience is students usually begin to work with the equipment and whilst I pretend not to hear questions such as 'What are we supposed to be doing?' I am watchful over what is happening. Students naturally begin to interact with the equipment, often working together, and soon start to make shapes and formulate questions.

After a few minutes of relatively free play, I ask them what they have been doing, and these responses typically occur:

✓ 'I've been trying to make all the numbers from 1 to 9.'
✓ 'I've been trying to make the letters of the alphabet.'
✓ 'We've been making star shapes.'

193

✓ 'I made a shape and my friend had to make a reflection of the shape.'

✓ 'I've been making triangles.'

✓ 'We've been making shapes that don't touch the middle pin.'

Because somebody inevitably says something about making different shapes, I build upon such a contribution by asking students to find all the possible triangles or quadrilaterals. Again, here is the issue of ownership of the problem growing from an idea students have already begun to think about.

I usually choose to pose the problem of finding all the different quadrilaterals slightly ambiguously in terms of whether rotations, reflections or translations 'count' as being different. These are key concepts I want to develop during a whole-class discussion later in the lesson. To initiate such discussion I ask individuals to come to the board and draw one of their shapes on the twenty or so nine-dot grids I have previously drawn on the board. If I have not had time to prepare the board before the lesson, I use my deftly honed skill of speedily drawing grids as students are working on their quadrilateral-finding task. This is typical of the competencies teachers develop under pressure! Projecting an image of these grids using an IWB is great (even for this Luddite).

Once we have a board full of contributions, I label each shape alphabetically and ask an open question about what anyone notices about the shapes. This inevitably provokes discussion about which shapes are the same or different, such as 'Shape C is the same as shape M' etc. Asking students to explain or justify their observations creates opportunities to develop concepts of congruence and similarity; likewise the use of vocabulary such as rotation, reflection and translation and enlargement. I will certainly guide discussion towards the properties of the shapes, in terms of equal length of sides, parallel sides and right angles.

This leads to naming and classifying the shapes. The issue of recording vocabulary and listing keywords is an aspect of making terminology explicit, usually followed up with a discussion about the meaning of certain words.

As the discussion develops, I rub out congruent shapes until we are left with a set of non-congruent quadrilaterals. Often a student will draw a triangle with a 'leg' hanging off a side or a corner. If this occurs, there exists an excellent opportunity to unpick a misconception about what defines a quadrilateral. If no such shape appears I will add one to the collection to ensure we have such a discussion. Another shape that frequently appears is a 'crossed quadrilateral". This can provide a useful focal point to discuss the differences between a 'normal' quadrilateral and one that has been drawn with four straight edges but by crossing over produces two triangles joined at a point. An extension task, to find and classify all the crossed quadrilaterals, provides a suitable challenge for some students.

Properties and names of shapes, angle, area and perimeter

If all 16 possible quadrilaterals have not been found, this could be the task for the next part of a lesson. I ask students to write any special properties and name each quadrilateral they draw. Other tasks based upon the shapes found could be to:

✓ determine the symmetries of each shape.
✓ draw shapes on enlarged grids so students can measure the angles with a protractor.
✓ work out the area of each shape (having established the area of the 1×1 square is one square unit).
✓ find how many congruent shapes there are for each quadrilateral.
✓ find the perimeter of each shape – there are three ways this might be done:
  – a) by measuring;
  – b) by algebraic coding (see diagram below); and, for post-Pythagoreans,
  – c) by writing the perimeter in surd form (I develop this later in the chapter).

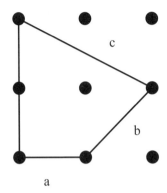

Writing the perimeter of each shape by using the defined lengths *a*, *b*, and *c* provides a purposeful context for collecting like terms: thus, the shape above has a perimeter of $3a + b + c$.

This idea can be worked on in reverse, i.e. Find quadrilaterals that have a perimeter of $2(a + c)$. As different shapes that have the same perimeter, though not necessarily the same area, can be drawn on the grid, this provides further opportunities to reinforce the absence of a connection between these concepts (unless of course we are considering perimeters and areas of regular polygons).

Finding all possible triangles

As well as finding all the possible quadrilaterals, students might be given the problem of finding all the possible triangles on a nine-dot grid and devising a systematic method to try to prove they have found them all. This problem can be extended to find all the triangles on a 16-dot grid and any systematic method students devised for a 9-dot grid can be applied to a 16-dot grid.

Every time a student measures an angle, calculates an area or describes a perimeter, he or she is naturally carrying out repetitive actions, and this is the basis of practise and consolidation.

Pythagoras, surds, trigonometry and rounding

On a nine-dot board there are five different lengths: (1, 2, $\sqrt{2}$, $2\sqrt{2}$ and $\sqrt{5}$). Post-Pythagorean students can therefore practise knowledge of surds, writing the length of each side and summing these to find the perimeter of each shape made. This idea can easily be developed so instead of leaving answers in surd form students can calculate perimeters of shapes to one decimal place. This creates an opportunity to deal with the issue of premature rounding (see the shape on the previous page). Both results of 6.6 and 6.7 might be produced, but only one, of course, is correct.

To practise trigonometry the following question might be posed: 'What size are the angles for each quadrilateral made on a nine-dot grid?'

To practise rounding, each angle can be calculated to one or two decimal places.

Vectors and equations of straight lines

To practise vectors: 'How many different vectors are there on a nine-pin geoboard?' This can be developed to consider how many vectors there are on 16-, 25-, 36-dot … grids. The problem can lead students to make a systematic collection to try to find all possible results. Such a task also creates the opportunity for students to recognise that for every vector there is another equal and opposite vector created by changing the polarity of the elements. Furthermore, there is a quadratic sequence to be found, connecting the size of the board with the total number of vectors. This provides an in-context problem for writing the nth term of the sequence so produced.

Other questions concerning vectors can be: 'Find all pairs of vectors that are perpendicular to each other on 9- or 16-pin geoboards.'

'What happens to the elements of a vector when it is rotated 90° clockwise or anticlockwise?'

To practise equations of straight lines the geoboard can be used as a coordinate grid and the questions 'How many different straight lines are there and what is the equation of each one?' can be posed. This is another useful problem particularly as there are 20 different equations of lines to be found and by extending the problem to a 16-dot grid there are between 50 and 60 solutions. There is also an interesting connection between this and the earlier problem about how many vectors there are on a 9-dot or a 16-dot grid.

A question such as 'Find all points which are not at a grid point when different pairs of straight lines cross' will engage students in solving equations simultaneously.

Finding the area of shapes whose vertices are not always on a pin will provide a suitable challenge for the higher-attaining students and two such problems are:

a) 'Calculate the intersecting area made when two triangles cross over.'
b) 'Calculate the area of a crossed quadrilateral.'

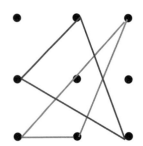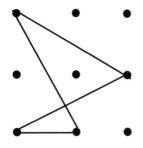

Seeking solutions to these final two problems may require students to draw upon a wide range of skills such as similarity, coordinates, equations of lines, solving simultaneous equations, calculating the distance between two points, applying the cosine rule and calculating the area of a triangle. Further questions can be constructed, and as each one is worked on there exist possibilities for students to practise, consolidate and develop their mathematics.

This wealth of mathematics for students to engage with has all been based upon a simple grid, some starting-point questions and some development tasks, with not a textbook in sight. We have not even begun to explore some of the problems arising from a 3x3x3-dot 3D grid: for example, how many 3D vectors there are and what cube dissections are possible.

However, it is time to leave geoboards and consider other areas of the curriculum where students can work without a textbook.

Setting up and solving simultaneous equations

One way of solving a pair of simultaneous equations is to set up a task where each student begins by knowing what the solutions for x and y are when written as a coordinate pair. The process can be constructed as follows:

1 Each student thinks of a pair of coordinates, e.g. (3, 11)
2 He or she then makes up two calculations where 3 is transformed into 11, for example $4 \times 3 - 1 = 11$ and $2 \times 3 + 5 = 11$.
3 Now each calculation is turned into an equation where the 3 is replaced by x and the 11 is replaced by y, for example $4x - 1 = y$ and $2x + 5 = y$.
4 Students give their pairs of equations to one another and in order for the 'swap over' to happen 'simultaneously' the class can be set a time limit for producing pairs of equations.
5 Students have to try to work out the values for x and y for each pair of equations they have received.
6 Students subsequently check each other's answers.

Students might use trial and improvement to work out the unknown values: in the first instance this is fine. Whether the teacher suggests other methods or asks students to invent their own methods is, of course, a decision for individual teachers to make. Some may suggest a graphical approach, while others may turn a pair of equations into a single equation, so using the above example students can try to solve:

$$4x - 1 = 2x + 5$$

This strategy combines three different ways for students to work: individually, in pairs and discussing ideas and methods in the whole group.

The next idea is initially based upon students working as a pair; the mathematical content is working with fractions. The only resource required is some brightly coloured paper, perhaps cut to A5 size.

Adding and subtracting fractions

Working in pairs, in order to discuss an idea or solve a problem jointly, is a strategy that can be used purposefully and to good effect with many tasks in a mathematics classroom. Sharing ideas to discuss something or combining information is a powerful way of enabling deeper study. To illustrate this, I offer tasks that focus on adding, subtracting and dividing fractions, carried out through paper-folding.

Each student is given a piece of A5 paper and is asked to fold it into thirds across the short side and into quarters across the long side to produce twelve twelfths:

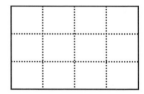

Holding a discussion about what happens, what size the individual pieces are and how they relate to the folds may be useful at this juncture. Asking students to confirm that thirds and quarters can be expressed as a number of twelfths is central to the next task.

This is to ask one student to fold the piece of paper into ⅔ of the original size and his or her partner to fold the piece into ¾ of the original size. Now comes the crux of the problem. I ask pairs of students to add their fractional pieces of paper together, i.e. ⅔ + ¾. Using the two pieces of paper we have:

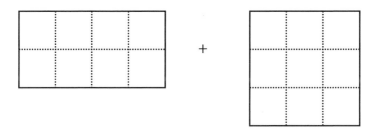

Given the student holding the ⅔ size will automatically have ⁸⁄₁₂ and the student with the ¾ will have ⁹⁄₁₂, the answer ¹⁷⁄₁₂ cannot be too far away from being realised. The same process can be used for carrying out subtraction, so ¾ − ⅔ becomes ⁹⁄₁₂ − ⁸⁄₁₂, producing the required answer of ¹⁄₁₂.

Of course, if the denominators of fractions to be added or subtracted are thirds and fifths, then the paper will need to be folded into three and five equal sections. The key issue is that a common denominator, though not necessarily the lowest, will always be created.

Dividing fractions and non-commutativity

To carry out a computation of ¾ ÷ ⅔, 'all' we have to do is to place the ¾ piece 'above' a division line and the ⅔ piece 'below' it. This might be enacted in a physical sense by asking one student to lend an arm, held out horizontally, and defining this as the division line. One student then holds the ⁹⁄₁₂ above and the other holds the ⁸⁄₁₂ piece below the division line. Using the folded pieces of paper we physically produce a situation with pieces of paper containing 9 pieces (twelfths) over (divided by) 8 pieces (twelfths), so producing the required answer of ⁹⁄₈. By inverting the calculation the answer of ⁸⁄₉ will be achieved. This may enable students to recognise that the process of division of fractions is not commutative.

Multiplying fractions and commutativity

Whereas addition, subtraction and division of fractions requires two pieces of paper, multiplication of fractions can be carried out using just one piece as follows:

1 Take a piece of paper that has been folded into twelve twelfths.
2 Fold this into three-quarters of the original size.
3 Now fold this piece into two thirds of its present size.

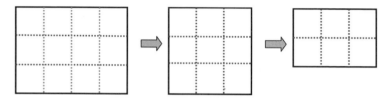

The resulting shape reveals ⁶⁄₁₂ or ½ of the original size. Reversing the order of the folds will obviously produce the same final outcome, and by doing this students can experience in a practical way the commutative property of multiplying fractions.

As indicated above, this approach does not always reveal the lowest common denominator. However, if students have been getting to grips with these different computations, recognising that certain values can be simplified should not be too complex a step to take.

Because the process is robust, students can try adding, subtracting, dividing and multiplying different pairs of fractions with any two denominators. Clearly, the physicality of the situation means that when the size of the denominator becomes large, say greater than ten, the folding process becomes tedious. The ultimate aim is for students to shift from the practical paper-folding situation to carry out pencil and paper or mental computations. Again, this shift from the concrete to the abstract will occur at a different rate for different students and is the basis of differentiated learning. Such decisions are navigated by students and negotiated by the classroom teacher, not by a textbook author.

As an extension, students can add pairs of fractions where both have a numerator of 1. The aim here is for students to see how the numbers connect together, thus leading to the generalisation for $1/a + 1/b$.

A more complex challenge is for students to try to generalise what happens when fractions of the form $a/b + c/d$ are added together. Here students have to carry out lots of calculations in order to seek a general result. This is different from students being given a procedure and applying it without understanding how the procedure works.

Alternative spending plans for department capitation

Not buying textbooks means departmental money can be used for many other purposes such as buying equipment, software licences, paying for the printing of a range of different grid papers and purchasing class sets of different types of calculators (simple, scientific, graphic). Every department can benefit from becoming institutional members of one or both professional associations for mathematics teaching: the Association of Teachers of Mathematics and the Mathematical Association. These associations produce marvellous journals and publications full of ideas for use in classrooms. Any departmental meeting could easily begin with an article from a journal as a stimulus for discussion.

The type of resources a department has available and the different ways they are used forms the pedagogical basis of a department and underpins the culture of what kind of things happen in mathematics lessons. If the central resource for a department is a textbook or a published scheme, and this guides teaching and learning in the department, this will have a significant impact upon departmental pedagogy.

PART 4

14

Mathematics and ...

In this chapter I fly a few kites and look at the possibility of broadening the scope of mathematics teaching with respect to parents, guardians and carers (PG&Cs), liaison with primary schools and engaging with mathematics in a mathematics department. I begin by looking at the feasibility of working with the PG&Cs of the students we teach.

Mathematics and PG&Cs

There is a strong case for prioritising time to work with adults, to share perspectives and help them make sense of some of the changes that take place in mathematics education. There are many positive benefits of opening classroom doors to show PG&Cs what happens and why it happens. This is all part of a process of transparency. Being honest, open and clear to parents about the departmental ethos has, in my experience, always been well rewarded in terms of the support that is offered in return. For example, when the department was intending to move towards all-ability teaching groups, I made it my business to explain to the parents of the potentially highest-achieving student why their child would not be disadvantaged as he began his GCSE course. The student subsequently had an article published in *Mathematics Teaching* (127). This demonstrated his capability to develop a problem that had been given to his all-ability GCSE class.

My experience reveals that seeking to rationalise why I teach mathematics the way I do and to communicate and justify this rationale to PG&Cs is an excellent way of self-checking the approaches I use and to strengthen my pedagogy. There are, however, more important reasons for working with PG&Cs and these are to build confidence in how their children are being taught mathematics, to help them understand why 'it was never like this when I was at school'!

Welcoming adults into mathematics classrooms so they can experience what their children typically do in school is central to organising 'Mathematics for PG&Cs' evenings in collaboration with school governors and/or the school Parent Teacher Association. I always found these to be extraordinarily positive events. Communicating the way a department teaches mathematics to PG&Cs is an important aspect of developing home–school relationships and fostering these can have particularly valuable outcomes. Each one of these events proved enjoyable, informative and, because of the different formats used, were always interesting and valuable.

Adults come to such events with a range of expectations about how their children should or ought to be taught mathematics and with issues about how much help they are able to support their children. Some may wish to discuss how they might best help their children when they 'cannot do their homework'. Adults have varying degrees of confidence in their own mathematical capability: some will relive the anxieties they felt when they were at school; others will be more confident. To try to cater for such a range, I have used different formats.

Whole-group introduction

One approach was to offer a task to reveal an important difference between the arithmetic of counting and the mathematics of pattern-spotting, predicting, conjecturing and generalising. The task I used works as follows:

1 On a piece of $1\,cm^2$ paper, draw a 7×7 cm square.
2 Starting from the top left-hand square, count one, two and three and colour in the fourth.
3 Now count again from the next (fifth) square, one, two, three and shade in the next square. (When the end of the first row

is reached, start again from the left-hand side of the next row down.)

4 Continue shading in every fourth square.

At some point during the counting and shading the pattern below emerges and can be described as [Grid 7, +4].

1	2	3	4	1	2	3
4	1	2				

The pattern is a set of diagonal lines and once recognised it is likely that shading by counting will be abandoned and shading according to the pattern will take over. At this point the counting stops and mathematics takes over.

Some developments are:

✓ Find the shading pattern for different rules using the same grid width.
✓ Change the width of the original grid to, say, size 8 and see what happens when different add rules are applied.
✓ Look for connections between add rules and grid widths.
✓ Classify common types of patterns.

This simple, accessible problem is an excellent demonstration of what is meant by 'working mathematically'.

A key feature is to cause PG&Cs to do some mathematics and, from this experience, discuss how their children engage with the subject. In a curriculum based upon problem-solving, it is incredibly easy to offer any number of problems to work on. However, I can imagine the reaction had I given them a textbook and invited them to 'work through exercise A on page 27'!

'Potted' versions of sequences of lessons

The idea behind this format is to offer some starting points for lessons that leads to developing mathematical thinking. There are umpteen ideas that might be used, and I offer three.

Routes on a grid

This idea is about finding all possible routes on a square-dot grid from the top left-hand corner point S to every other point on the grid. Normally, as a starting point (say with a Year 7 class), there could be some discussion about how many different routes there are if there were no rules. At some point, by introducing or discussing the need to reduce the number of ways of moving, to Right and Down, a more systematic collection of routes can be found leading to the following result.

S●	1●	1●	1●
1●	2●	3●	4●
1●	3●	6●	10●
1●	4●	10●	20●

These are, of course, numbers from Pascal's Triangle arrangement (although this array of numbers was known in India and China long before Pascal), and the diagram needs to be turned through 45° to view the arrangement in its usual format. Given the enormous importance of Pascal's Triangle and the number of places it arises in various guises in mathematics, the value of introducing this idea early in children's mathematical experience cannot be understated. Consequently, this is a valuable way of helping adults see mathematics as a collection of connected ideas.

Predicting values on 5 × 5 and 6 × 6 grids opens up one way of looking for and developing the arrangement. Once the values are established there are many number patterns that can be found and explored. This creates opportunities to demonstrate how a seemingly simple, accessible starting point can be developed, thus catering for the different mathematical aspirations of children.

Some speedy data-handling

This task is so beautifully simple yet it engages everyone in using and applying a range of data-handling skills. The lesson begins by projecting an image of a star sheet from page 9 of the ATM publication *Learning and Teaching Mathematics without a Textbook* (Ollerton, 2002) for no more than 10 seconds. With the image hidden, I ask everyone to individually write an estimate of how many stars they think they saw. I collect the answers writing each estimate on the board. This takes no more than a couple of minutes.

Next I ask them to think about different ways we might use this data to agree upon a value that is representative of the data. Inevitably, different types of averages emerge: the mean, the median and the mode. Finding the value halfway between the largest and the smallest estimate is often a surprisingly accurate method. Of course, the data could be illustrated in the form of a grouped frequency graph or a pie chart. Again, there is a beautiful simplicity in setting up a task that holds so much opportunity for developing statistical thinking.

If a second estimate is requested, perhaps after another brief viewing of the star sheet image, this usually produces a decrease in the size of the range as more people tend to make a second estimate closer to the previously calculated averages.

A workshop of ideas

A workshop of ideas involves setting out different problems written on separate pieces of coloured card around a classroom together with various resources and types of grid papers. The visual impact of walking into a classroom with lots of equipment, coloured paper and different grids creates an excellent flavour of what working in a mathematics classroom is like. When using a workshop-style format adults are invited to spend approximately one hour working on typical problems. Having a range of problems, puzzles and games of varying complexity means everyone can find something to work on. In this more relaxed atmosphere adults can have informal discussions about the nature of the work and how the ideas are intended to help their children become active problem-solvers.

Typical examples of ideas are:

Make all the different solid cuboids from 24 linking cubes. For each calculate its surface area. What do you notice?	*Write the multiples of 9 until you see a pattern. Make a note of other patterns you find in the multiples of 9.*

Find a way of working out the average shoe size of everyone in the room. Draw a picture to illustrate your work.	*Draw a graph of the multiples of 2. What does a graph of one more than the multiples of 2 look like?*

Make all the different shapes by joining 5 squares together edge to full edge. Describe the symmetry of each shape.	*Think of a number, add 5, double the result, take away 9 then subtract the number you first thought of. What happens? Why?*

Place each of the numbers 1, 2, 3, 4, 5, 6, 7, 8 and 9 in a 3 by 3 square so that each line of three numbers adds up to the same total.	*If 16 is always the 'answer' make up some questions. Use different numbers and types of operations.*

Plenary

Bringing everyone together to share perceptions is a key part of such events especially if ideas have been worked on in different classrooms. One part of the plenary can be used to invite PG&Cs to discuss what they have been doing. This approach is a way of modelling how PG&Cs might similarly discuss with their children what they have been doing at school.

Those PG&Cs for whom mathematics may be a mystery usually value discussion about how they can help their children. A useful approach is for PG&Cs to ask questions that gently encourage their children to explain what they have been doing. Quite often such questioning can be the catalyst for a child to make sense of something he or she may be stuck on, purely as an outcome of trying to verbalise that stuckness.

Of course, such approaches to questioning are skills teachers build up over a lifetime so we cannot expect PG&Cs to become expert questioners overnight. The important issue is opening up the possibility, and the importance, of asking questions per se. Again, this is a part of opening up mutual home–school support. An interesting aspect of such events is how frequently PG&Cs are often more concerned with trying to reach a solution to a problem they have worked on earlier in the evening than anything else: somehow the mathematics overtakes other concerns. It is almost as though the challenge of figuring something out, of solving a puzzle, creates its own momentum. I am not particularly surprised by such responses, as they demonstrate the power of puzzlement as a strong motivator for learning.

At one evening PG&Cs became so deeply engaged in the mathematics that at the end of the evening, as they were leaving, I had to remind them we had not yet discussed the 'main' issues relating to the then latest government's change to the curriculum. Given the mathematical buzz in the room, this did not seem important.

The more information PG&Cs have about how their children are encouraged to learn mathematics, the greater the possibility of sharing perspectives, encouraging openness, gaining valuable support and finding common ground. Nurturing PG&Cs'

confidence that the department's teaching methods are sound, carefully considered and appropriately applied to their children's mathematical development is of paramount importance.

Mathematics and cross-phase liaison

What kind of information do secondary school teachers want or need about the children they are going to teach for the first time? What quantity of information will a teacher have time to read, take cognisance of and use to plan lessons? What kind of information can a secondary school teacher realistically make use of? Questions such as these might be a focus for a primary teacher to consider with regard to the information he or she provides and how it will benefit the children and their future secondary school teachers. Just how much time primary teachers put into the records they write and to what extent such information is used by secondary school colleagues is similarly worth considering ... perhaps before such records are compiled in the future.

Of greater importance than the quantity of information is sharing the ways children are taught and how children experience learning in different phases. Having spent my first two years teaching in a primary school, I always find it refreshing to visit primary classrooms. I always gain a vibrant sense of interesting environments, where walls are plastered with wonderful, colourful displays and classrooms are stimulating places.

On one occasion I was invited to do some cross-phase mathematics liaison with a local primary school and was acutely reminded of the responsibility and autonomy young children are encouraged to develop. This was exemplified during a lesson on scale drawing. I set up a situation where pairs of children drew an outline of each other on the back of old sheets of wallpaper and used this outline to take measurements of height, arm length, leg length, shoulder width, and so on. The main aim was to make quarter-size scale models of themselves: the mathematics was measuring and quartering (halving and halving again).

After a few minutes one girl asked me if she could put all her information on to a spreadsheet. At this point I looked around for the class teacher to see what the procedure was for using 'the computer'. The girl, however, stopped me in my tracks when she glibly said she knew how to use a spreadsheet and the children in her class used the computer whenever they needed to! Gobsmacked, I marvelled at her sense of independence and her teacher's methodology, which clearly encouraged such behaviour and expected the children to work in this way.

Having such insights can only have a positive effect upon one's teaching, particularly recognising the kind of learning environments primary-aged children are used to and the degree of responsibility they are encouraged to take. Of course, the nature of secondary-phase education means students are taught in separate subjects for most of the time. This has a significant impact because children move from teacher to teacher, each with their different expectations. However, some secondary schools make use of more integrated approaches, combining certain subjects for the first year of secondary school. Other schools seek to minimise the number of staff who teach the new intake, thus creating a situation where fewer teachers have a greater knowledge of the students.

With regard to mathematics, creating learning environments where greater emphasis is put upon the creation of display work, student presentations and students producing their own 'topic' booklets will help, in part, to bridge the primary–secondary transfer.

Many years ago I attended an ATM branch meeting in Blackpool where the keynote speaker, Peter Lacey, asked the audience to sit together in small cross-phase primary/secondary groups to discuss aspects of their teaching. The quality and nature of the ensuing discussions was most revealing with regard to mathematical content and the relative degrees of independence the primary teachers encouraged in their children … which somehow seemed to disappear over the summer holiday!

Mathematics and mathematics teachers

Sometimes I prioritise my time to do some mathematics, although this does not happen as often as I would like. This is hardly surprising, given the busy and multi-faceted nature of the job of teaching. However, when I actually engage in some mathematics I revisit my own enjoyment of the discipline and this reminds me why I teach it. I strengthen my rationale for teaching and this inevitably means I can take refreshed enthusiasms with me into my classrooms.

Involvement in a Professional Association

Creating opportunities to work on mathematics and share this experience with others might be considered an unaffordable luxury, a rarity. An important influence on my mathematical and pedagogical development has occurred as a result of being an active member of the ATM. I have learnt a great deal by working with other members, through curriculum working groups, regional conferences and branch meetings. There is also the annual Easter Conference, when I devote four days to working on mathematics and mathematics education and catching up with other members of the association. I engage in the pleasures of problem-solving and the thrill of exercising those mathematically rusty parts of my brain.

Over the years I have attended many interesting sessions and have worked on hundreds of problems, which I have subsequently adapted in my teaching. Populating schemes of work with ideas I have worked on has added richness and variety to my bank of ideas. I have already mentioned the Dance and Mathematics session I attended and what a powerful experience this proved to be in Chapter 7. I always went to sessions run by Lyndon Baker and Ian Harris, though sadly Ian has now passed away. In a session in 2003 the group was presented with the following problem:

$$(115)^2 = 11 \times 12[25]$$

The 25 in the square brackets in the calculation emerges from 5^2, which forms the tens and the units digits when combined with

216

the product formed by calculating 11 × 12. Thus the complete answer becomes 13 225.

We were invited to see if this always worked and this led me to question why it worked. The problem can be developed to see what happens when we square numbers ending in a 6, a 7 or any digit, and I worked on this with another person (Sam). As we began to make sense of what happened and why the result occurred, we became more and more intrigued. We developed the task to prove why it worked and what mathematical adjustments would be needed if the unit digit were something other than a 5. However, in order to solve the problem, to reach an end point, we chose not to work on any of the other problems Ian and Lyndon kept offering the group. There are issues here, which I develop below.

Time to reflect

Finding time to reflect upon certain issues is not always easy. All too often, as teachers, we have to move on to the next task without having time to take breath. Reflecting upon what we have been doing to determine what the implications might be for future action can be highly problematic. Yet it is only when we reflect upon something we open up the possibility of making changes to how we think and, therefore, to change how we teach.

The experience of being a learner helps confirm the importance of having choice, especially regarding the pace I worked at; of being able to negotiate what I worked on; and, most importantly, not being hurried along to finish something at the teacher's pace. If 'pace' in a mathematics classroom is construed as a whole class 'moving on' to the next idea at the speed at which this is intended to happen, then I have many concerns about the effect of pace upon students' development. Learners need time to work on ideas, to tackle problems in different depths. They need time to think about and sort out ideas for themselves. If pace is seen as acceleration, I suggest we consider the impact upon deep learning. I believe there is a strong case for actively slowing pupils

217

down, so they reflect upon what they have learnt and go deeper into concepts: to understand the 'why' behind the 'how' and the 'what' is crucial.

Doing some mathematics at department meetings

As a young teacher, I remember Eric Love, my head of department, starting a meeting by casting a whole lot of ATM MATs (see Chapter 5) on the table and inviting colleagues to discuss what mathematics they might be able to get out of them. For the first 15 or so minutes we 'played' with the equipment and discussed the potential for using them in our teaching. On other occasions we considered what use we could make of other types of equipment, such as linking cubes. Discussing mathematics for the first part of a meeting and developing curriculum ideas for modules within the departmental scheme of work was something we did. This produced a collaborative and evolutionary approach to curriculum development which all members of the department had some responsibility for and ownership of.

Having such opportunities to discuss mathematics at the beginning of a meeting was a marvellous way of sharing different teaching approaches. This also meant business agenda items were appropriately relegated to matters of secondary importance. Seeking a balance between curriculum development opportunities and the need to get through the business agenda is a critical issue for heads of department to consider. One aspect of this is to decide how much departmental business can be conducted outside department meetings. The greater the resolve we have about effective ways of teaching mathematics and the ways we seek to build effective learning environments is all part of professional development. This is something departments can do first and foremost in-house. Using departmental meetings to exchange individual enthusiasms, share expertise and excitement for the subject and discuss lesson ideas that worked is fundamental to professional development. This can be achieved by doing some mathematics.

Prioritising time to work on mathematics can, however, be difficult, particularly when there are so many new initiatives showering down upon schools from central government and local authorities. Schools becoming academies, tests to be taught to and targets to be 'met' can, if we let them, have a substantial and damaging impact upon how mathematics is taught and learnt. Whenever prescription from 'above' starts to run counter to a department's thoughtfully considered and soundly constructed pedagogy, we need to utilise skills and find the strength to resist unhelpful pressures. I firmly believe in honest and open argument, and if this fails moving towards a state of healthy disrespect and, if absolutely necessary, gentle subversion.

15

Doing less of the two more boring parts of teaching

In this chapter I consider some accepted orthodoxies regarding teaching and learning mathematics in schools and explore the possibilities of working differently. I discuss alternative ways of working, not to offer change for the sake of change, but to consider how some changes can 'create time' by spending less time on certain other tasks. In particular, I look at marking habits and implications for setting homework.

Marking books, marking time: 'traditional' marking is a bit of a bind

One of the more boring aspects of being a mathematics teacher must surely be taking home armfuls of students' exercise books for marking. In my experience this is one of the biggest yawns imaginable ... washing up, by comparison, is an exciting and creative activity. Spending time putting ticks and kisses against students' answers and possibly adding a brief comment seems futile and never convinced me of the value of what I was doing. At issue is why we feel the need to do it? Is this yet another issue of other people controlling our teaching so we are seen to be doing the job properly?

Here are a couple of rhetorical questions:

1 Do these 'other people' still have several armfuls of marking to do?
2 Is marking something we do for PG&Cs, Ofsted or to enhance our students' learning?

I often felt, when marking books, it would have been far more valuable if I had been able to say something to each student, particularly when it appeared some had made a simple error and others had seemingly lost the plot altogether ... perhaps it was more a case of them losing my plot or it made little sense to them. Worse still were feelings I must have been speaking in another language, though given mathematics has its own language, perhaps I was. Even worse was a deep-down feeling that students would pay little if any attention to my marking. This added to the sense of the meaninglessness of the turgid task and the time I spent in my state of futility. It is useful, therefore, to consider what kind of marking is worth doing if it is to have value and impact upon students' development.

This issue came strongly into focus during a whole-school InSET day many years ago when staff looked at a small sample of students' exercise books from different subject areas. The main intention was to gain a wider perspective on the types of tasks students experienced in different colleagues' subject areas. My attention, however, was taken by comments written by different teachers to one student. The student did not have a statement of special educational need; however, she did find academic work a struggle. To my shock, I found very few supportive or positive comments. Such was my concern at what I read that I noted down some of the comments (I have not included comments such as 'date' and 'heading', which also frequently appeared). The comments below are an accurate picture of what was written in her books:

Incomplete.

Very untidy, poor homework.

More observations should have been made.

Untidy *∂!?+*!*$ [ironically, this second word was illegible].

Late – no work.

Writing untidy.

I cannot read some of this work.

You've missed the point.

Spellings. Spellings.

Good so far.

There are so many bad spellings.
Your spelling is awful.
Better here, slightly.
Very poor spellings.
You silly person.
Good idea, poor spelling.
Untidy.
You've absolutely wasted your time, then.
Messy.
Spellings.

The outcome for me was profound and deeply disturbing. Gaining this wider picture of the kind of comments being written had a direct impact upon my practice. This was to avoid writing such comments in the future and to become more acutely aware of how such comments might appear to students. The effect such comments might have upon the student was worth considering, and I formulated some questions:

✓ Did this student know she was not very good at spelling?
✓ What would you think of these comments if you were the girl's parent?
✓ What value do such comments have in supporting learning?
✓ Was writing such comments an effective use of teachers' time?
✓ Is this experience similar for teachers in other schools?

I would be very surprised if the student did not know she had severe difficulties with spelling. Yet how would such comments help her improve? This would clearly require time and support. However, if a teachers' valuable time is taken up with writing such comments, this is not only a waste of time, but also a lost opportunity to create a more encouraging climate for the student to improve her spelling.

If similar occurrences happen in other schools and if little advantage is gained by students or by teachers, it is worth considering who benefits from this kind of marking. More importantly, what kind of marking and feedback promotes achievement?

One of the more important aspects of teaching is lesson planning. The more interesting ideas we come up with the more interested our students are likely to be. Planning lessons must also take account of the ways we expect students to work both inside and outside the classroom and the different ways we want students to demonstrate their learning. Some outcomes could be for students to produce a poster, do a write-up or make a PowerPoint presentation. When a sequence of lessons is planned with the intention of developing in-depth understanding and where different students are expected to achieve different end-points, this inevitably has an impact upon the type of homework students might be encouraged to do ... I feel a confession coming on.

Confession time

As a form tutor, I was often aware of some students copying each other's homework answers. This would probably be to meet a deadline of handing in their exercise books during registration. I confess I never prevented such behaviour, mainly because I was more concerned about the futility of taking such actions and whether or not it was my role to police when or where students did their homework (or copied it from someone else!). I was equally conscious I did not wish my relationship with my tutees to be undermined or affected by demands made upon them by colleagues' methods of organisation. This may appear unsupportive of colleagues' efforts ... but a confession is, after all, about being honest.

Those students who had not completed their homework the previous evening (or that morning on the school bus) were clearly only wanting to play the game to avoid a sanction. All too often I felt I had to set homework not to enhance students' learning but because this was the school policy or because someone had received a complaint about their child not having any homework over a period of time. However, suppose a school policy actually gets in the way of effective learning? What if a policy leads teachers to setting off-the-cuff, unplanned tasks are more for the sake of fulfilling the policy than for the benefit of students? What if a policy is no more than window-dressing for senior management, for PG&Cs or the impending arrival of Ofsted? My concern is that homework can take on a disproportionate dimension and be a root cause of conflict between teachers and students, adolescents and PG&Cs, culminating in the cry from the kitchen: 'Have you done your homework yet? ... You're not going out until ...' (A door is heard closing with a loud bang.)

Homework, homogeneity and heuristics

Whether homework is intended to extend or develop the work students are doing, whether it is used for practise, consolidation or revision purposes or to collect information for use in a future lesson, the central issue is about the kind of homework tasks that will complement classwork. However this can be difficult as we cannot predict what different students will achieve in a lesson. Of course we have moments in lessons when setting an unplanned though connected task suddenly seems far more appropriate than the one we may have anticipated, just as sometimes we come up with an inspirational idea as we walk down the corridor to a lesson.

In any class there are going to be wide variations in students' home backgrounds, the support systems they have at home and the love and encouragement they are given. As such, any work we ask students to do outside school needs to acknowledge such differences exist. This requires care and sensitivity both in terms of tasks posed and our expectations of what anyone might achieve. Some schools offer homework clubs either at lunchtime or after school. Such initiatives are positive ways of supporting students.

Below are examples of homework tasks likely to gain different responses and which will not require any formal marking beyond the recognition that students have had a go:

1   Find out about the Fibonacci Sequence.
2   Make a list of everything you know about quadrilaterals.

3 Count how many electrical appliances there are at home.

4 Find out how good your mum, dad or guardian is at long multiplication, long division or solving algebraic equations.

5 Keep a record of how much television you watch over a week.

6 Keep a record of how much time you spend playing computer games over a week.

7 Keep a record of how long you spend on Facebook or Twitter over a week.

8 Keep a record of who does the household chores during a typical week.

9 Explain to someone at home something you have learnt in mathematics today.

10 Draw a map of your journey from school to home.

11 Find out about different counting systems.

12 Make a poster on a piece of A4 paper to describe something you have understood about the work we had been doing in today's lesson.

Example 4) frequently causes some amusement as well as creating conditions for home–school dialogue. In response to 11), as well as receiving counting systems from different historical periods and in different languages, somebody once came back with the 'yan, tan, tethera …', a system for counting sheep. The poster resulting from 12) can form an 'instant' display (I develop this later in the chapter).

Each of these tasks can be developed in the next lesson so instead of homework being a continuation of something from a lesson it becomes preparation work for the next. Homework can be used for ongoing writing-up purposes to cause learners to be explicit about what they are working on. Teaching in ways that does not generate a plethora of answers to narrow questions means adopting a different style of marking and feedback, which I describe below.

Writing comments in response to students' work

To decide what kind of marking helps students become better mathematicians and better learners, it is useful to consider how any form of marking is likely to have a positive impact upon learning. One approach I found purposeful was to write lengthy comments (50 to 100 words). This might sound a time-consuming task. Yet because I only collected students' work in once every three or four weeks this meant I redesigned my marking by writing formative comments and providing feedback. On some occasions this would be quite detailed, as illustrated in the second comment below. Collecting in students' work every three of four weeks, though, did not mean I only saw each student's work every three or four weeks. During lessons I regularly made short written comments, perhaps suggesting something a student might try next. In this way I kept myself informed of students' ongoing progress while setting realistic agreed targets during lessons. Below is a typical comment to Jane, a Year 10 student who had made considerable progress.

There is some good work here, Jane, and further evidence that you are developing sound work habits that will help you achieve your potential in this subject. There are a couple of small errors you could apply a brain cell or two to; however, this apart, you have achieved a good understanding of the ideas involved in transformations. You have again written a useful set of final thoughts and these are a further indication of the ideas you have understood. They also help me determine the kind of tasks I need to offer you in future to help you develop your mathematical thinking. I hope you told your Mum what a great cardigan I thought she knitted for you!

This next comment is a response to some trigonometry work a Year 11 student did. On this occasion the module had lasted for five weeks, and while trigonometry was the central concept students worked on a whole range of interconnected skills, from rounding up to a number of decimal places to drawing graphs of sine functions. Kelly was a hardworking student who put a great deal of time into her work outside lessons.

Extracts from Kelly's write-up appear in the former ATM journal *Micromath* (Autumn 1995, pp9–11).

Another super piece of work, Kelly, again showing the depth of thought that you have taken your ideas to. Every aspect of your final write-up shows a careful approach. Your analysis of sine functions is really good and this level of mathematics takes the assessment of your work off the scale (at the higher end!). You have set up and solved your own problems in order to work out lengths and angles in right-angled triangles. The further work using a clinometer clearly caused you some problems that you were able to engage with after some thought. Your final section really says it all. I find what you have written here very interesting indeed because you have clearly set out what you have gained and understood from this trigonometry project. I like the way you have described the need to use a calculator for carrying out a calculation as opposed to speeding up a calculation. So this is another excellent piece of work and looking to the future it will obviously be important that you can recognise when and how to use these skills in examinations. Now then, what can I nag you about?

Because I put this kind of concerted energy into providing feedback, I made a point, when returning work, to ask students to read carefully what I had written. Sometimes I asked them to write a comment in response. If an opportunity arose to engage with students in an amusing way, perhaps by mentioning something related to a recent event, I might choose to add something of such a nature. Thus my mention of Jane's cardigan in the first comment, which arose from a discussion I'd had with her mother at a recent consultation evening.

An outcome of word processing my comments (initially on a bright-green-screen Amstrad) was I also had a record of what I had written and was able to store and recall comments when necessary. Such an *aide-mémoire* meant great when writing summative reports.

This type of feedback developed as a direct consequence of the portfolios students created for GCSE; an approach that filtered down into Key Stage 3. Students usually wrote up three or four extended pieces of work each term and this had a direct bearing upon the nature of the planning as outlined in Chapter 10.

Tasks that won't require so much marking

Below are some suggestions about the kinds of tasks that can reduce the quantity of marking whilst providing students with a rich, more varied diet in mathematics lessons.

Students producing posters

Posters provide students with opportunities to demonstrate what they know as well as helping enhance the classroom environment. Posters can be created out of just about any work students do and, as such, it is not necessary for them to be pristine or time-consuming to produce. Indeed, putting up displays about ongoing ideas to stimulate discussion is equally as valuable as posters produced when a topic is completed. Displays can be used as a focus for discussion, to help develop students' understanding of a concept.

For example, some work on trigonometric functions might proceed as follows. Each pair of students is given a sheet of graph paper with $y = \sin x$ already drawn on it. They are then asked to draw just one of the following graphs, superimposing it on the graph paper supplied:

$y = 2\sin x$, $y = \frac{1}{2}\sin x$, $y = \sin 2x$, $y = \sin\frac{1}{2}x$,
$y = 2\sin 2x$, $y = 2\sin\frac{1}{2}x$, $y = \frac{1}{2}\sin 2x$, $y = \frac{1}{2}\sin\frac{1}{2}x$

Once such a collection of graphs has been produced and displayed, students can discuss the similarities and the differences between the graphs. The main intention is to develop students' understanding of how the period and the amplitude of the different trigonometric functions compare. Of greater importance is how students can form generalities about the impact of a and b for functions of the form $a\sin bx$.

This strategy of asking students to produce information for a whole-class discussion by creating an instant display can be applied to most or all areas of the mathematics curriculum. Other examples are:

✓ exploring linear and quadratic graphs;
✓ drawing all the possible cuboids made from a fixed number of cubes;
✓ collaboratively writing out all the divisors of the numbers from 1 to 100;
✓ producing all the possible vectors on a defined size of grid;
✓ collaboratively producing the consecutive sums for different numbers.

The idea behind such 'instant' display work is to draw out relationships within the concept under consideration. A secondary issue here is about cutting down on marking – when students are producing work for display they are not producing work for me to mark.

Student presentations

If students come to expect they will present some aspect of mathematics to their peers and at the same time learn to listen to each other, presentations can become a powerful aspect of learning mathematics. Leading up to a presentation, students might make a poster or produce a PowerPoint about what they have learnt. While presentations might usually be seen as the culmination of a topic, this need not always be the case. For example, if on the spur of the moment one notices a student has, perhaps for the first time, understood a concept other students may benefit from hearing, he or she could be encouraged to give a short explanation to demonstrate this newfound understanding. I recall asking one student to make a poster to explain the convention for rounding up a value to two-decimal places when it appeared he had understood this process for the first time.

Students setting and marking tests for each other

Imagine a scenario where you have been working with a Year 10 class on the central concept of Pythagoras' Theorem. Now consider the following process:

✓ Ask pairs of students who usually work at the same pace and achieve similar levels of understanding to write test questions for each other – say three or four questions to last for approximately twenty or so minutes.

✓ Each student works out answers and prepares a mark scheme. The teacher's role during this part of the process is to check the kind of questions produced and monitor them for comprehension and fairness.

✓ At the beginning of the next lesson, students do each others' test questions.

✓ At the end of the test students swap papers and, using their prepared mark schemes, mark each other's answers.

Not only are students learning how to answer questions on a specific concept area, they are also learning how to ask and mark questions. This is valuable preparation for doing examinations in a more formal setting. Furthermore, because we learn by asking questions as well as knowing how to answer them, this is a valuable process. If students learn to pose questions about a concept, this must mean they have an idea of what the concept is about. Such a process does require the teacher to observe and record what happens, but does not require the teacher to take any marking home.

I am mindful in writing this chapter that I may appear critical both of the kinds of practices that occur in some schools and of the underlying reasons for such practices. This is certainly not my aim. The main intention is to consider different ways we might operate with regard to marking and feedback, the nature of planning and the kind of homework tasks set for students. If we spend too much time doing tick/kiss marking we cannot spend sufficient time planning interesting lessons, which has an impact upon how students perceive mathematics.

The more interested our students are by what we plan, the better they are likely to respond; the better they respond, the more they will understand; the more they understand, the better they are going to behave ... everything is connected.

16

And finally ... working in all-attainment groups where 'everything is connected'

In this chapter I consider one of the most complex and omnipotent issues regarding how children experience mathematics. It is something where everything becomes connected and is about how children are grouped in order to learn mathematics. Specifically, I raise questions about how and why decisions are taken to form separate teaching groups according to notions of students' 'ability'. I strongly and unequivocally argue by actively deciding not to create so-called ability groups and instead making positive decisions to teach all children in mixed-ability groups we can best support every student.

When young people's learning is dominated by judgements of ability, their sense of identity may be profoundly affected, not just while they are at school, but beyond, into adulthood. Hart et al (2004, 4)

The power of expectation and the dangers of comparison

At the heart of human endeavour is the all-encompassing effect of expectation, both by self and by others, has upon achievement. Self-expectation is fundamental to self-identity, to how we gauge our present accomplishments and to the targets we set ourselves for future aspirations and goals. This is true whether we are in a learning situation, digging the garden, writing or going for a jog.

Several years ago I 'lurched' around the Fairfield Horseshoe in the Lake District in a most disappointing time in comparison to those I had previously achieved. One week later I did the same route and knocked 20 minutes off. On each occasion I had expectations of how long it should take, and each time I set myself targets to aspire to. Had I tried to compete against some of those maniacal fell-runners who complete the course in unbelievable times, I would probably have stayed at home and got out a jigsaw. Comparing myself to such athletes would have been nonsensical.

Some years later with dodgy knees and a heart complaint my enjoyment of the fells has changed – I am now a careful uphill plodder. However, the same motivation of getting to the top with my best pal, to see the view, to enjoy butties and a flask of coffee in the beauty of being out in the hills remains. I gain inordinate pleasure from whatever I can achieve. What is important here is not to compare myself to others and certainly not to concern myself with comparisons made by others. I can do nothing about comparisons other people may choose to make.

In classrooms, creating situations that cause children to compare themselves with each other is to detract from the more important business of personal achievement. Of course, children do compare themselves to one another and soon find out who is the fastest, the cleverest, the wittiest, the richest and the poorest. As adults we neither have to subscribe to this nor encourage it. By creating ability sets we are, however, creating a potentially damaging culture based upon comparison. Children inevitably form opinions about what expectations they believe their teachers have of them and the set a child is placed in sends clear messages about what these are. Whether we encourage it or not or like it or not, children talk about the 'dumbos' in the low sets and the 'swots' in the high sets. Yet we cannot separate emotional factors of learning from cognitive aspects of learning; how we feel about what we do impacts upon the quality of the outcomes we achieve.

Suffice to say, if students constantly receive subliminal messages about how 'good' or how 'weak' they are, according to the set number they are allocated, this will directly impact upon students' responses and behaviours in the present and achievements in the future. The expectations that teachers form of students' achievements are similarly crucial. The most potent type of expectations are those are realistic and co-constructed with students.

However, if a teacher's expectations are framed by the ability group a student is placed in or are arrived at by comparison to other students in the class, then I have grave concerns about the impact such comparisons may have.

How a teacher communicates his or her expectations will impact upon the ideas students form about themselves and, therefore, upon their achievements. If the culture of a classroom is about students not being compared to each other then we set up a useful form of competition, of students competing with their personal best. In such a culture, targets are negotiated and agreed between the individual student and the teacher. Expectations and targets can be challenging yet realistic. Targets, however, must be tangible.

My experience of teaching mathematics in both setted and mixed-ability groups leads me to the strong conviction that not only is the latter by far the most rewarding and intellectually challenging way to teach mathematics, it is also the most mathematically enabling and socially just form of organisation within which children learn mathematics. Learning in mixed-ability teaching groups is an issue of inclusion; of social justice.

Having experienced the ignominy of being taught in a bottom stream myself between the ages of 11 and 14 I have a good insight into what this feels like. Indeed, reading Daniel Pennac's *School Blues* (translated in 2010) has interesting resonances. As an adult I can articulate what impact bottom-set experiences had upon self-esteem. I do not need theories or research data to understand what being in the bottom set is like: I know what it's like and it's not nice. I also know what it is like to have to gain self-respect amongst my peers by being expert at being 'bad'; that gaining kudos when academic avenues had been cut off meant finding other, non-academic ways of showing my mettle. How I subsequently aspired to become a teacher, a head of mathematics and a senior lecturer is unimportant. What is important is being in a small minority of mathematics teachers who have personally experienced life in the 'bottom' class. I speak, therefore, with some authority and much personal insight.

Developing my self-esteem as a 14-year-old 'mathematician'

How we help students develop self-esteem as learners – of anything – is clearly an important consideration. How students in 'bottom' sets, however, are helped to build their self-esteem is a highly complex issue, particularly if the very system of setting is a contributory factor to esteem being boosted or undermined.

This was certainly the case for me in my early teens when I was provided with a diet of very boring mathematics – a replication of the work I had done in my primary years and continued to be so into the third year of my secondary schooling. Lessons were about boredom and frustration. The only lifeline was playing football, frequently picking the teams by passing a note around in a lesson before break so we did not have to waste our own valuable time. Jackets down, goals marked out, teams lined up and off we'd go. Bliss.

One lesson, however, for some unknown reason, Mr Green, a PE teacher who taught the Year 9 bottom set for mathematics, taught us something markedly different from the kind of mathematics we had previously been used to: solving simultaneous equations. I didn't know why I was solving these equations or what they were for, but I knew this 'algebra' work, which involved xs and ys, was what pupils in the top set did. I therefore felt to be doing something really boffin-like. Then a really important thing happened – I could do them. I was, therefore, doing 'top-set' mathematics. Discovering I was capable of doing the kind of work other pupils in higher sets were doing was a significant realisation and a significant boost to my self-esteem. Furthermore, I could use algebra to check my answers and know whether I had worked them out correctly. I remember the power of being able to do some 'really hard' (top-set) mathematics. That evening, quite voluntarily, I solved 50 or 60 simultaneous equations, filling page after page of my exercise book with their solutions. The next day I could barely wait for the maths lesson to begin so I could show Mr Green what I had achieved. I was bursting with pride. Upon deeper reflection, it was Mr Green who provided me with access to mathematics. He was the person who offered me the joy of real success and the confidence to feel I could do it. I had achieved success at a level beyond the expectations of myself and my teachers. I firmly believe this event had a profound impact upon my development. This, perhaps, was my first encounter with the entitlement curriculum. Yet I have never worked out why Mr Green decided one day to teach the bottom set as though they were the top set ... perhaps he saw no reason why not to!

Setting, social class and politics

Setting students by measures of perceived 'ability', as a form of creating teaching groups, mirrors aspects of our UK society. These are the class distinctions that pervade daily life in some shape or form and they impact upon the causes of inequality. That a class system exists cannot be denied. In his article in the *TES*, 'Little Improvement in the Lot of the Poor' (29 April, 2005), Peter Wilby (editor of the *New Statesman*) offered the following: 'for compulsory education, the biggest policy priority should be to create, in each school, a mix of abilities and home backgrounds that comes as close as possible to the mix in the general population'. This was a timely suggestion and whether this system should be perpetuated in our schools in the guise of students' needs and how best they can be provided for, through setting by ability, is something teachers can decide to do something about.

Sukhnandan and Lee (1988, 43) in their review of research offer the following: 'homogeneous forms of grouping reinforce segregation of pupils in terms of social class gender, race and age (season of birth). Consequently, low-ability classes often contain a disproportionately large number of pupils from working-class backgrounds, boys, ethnic minorities and summer-born children.' Mirroring forms of elitism in terms of class, gender, race and age can surely not be considered a humanitarian basis for our mathematical education system, yet one has to look far and wide to find many mathematics departments teaching in mixed-attainment groups beyond Year 7.

Mike Askew's (Professor of Education, King's College, London) closing speech to delegates at the 6th British Congress of Mathematics Education (BCME) conference (University of Warwick, 2005) gave support to mixed-attainment teaching, noting in Finland grouping by ability was abolished 25 years ago. Indeed, the Finnish system of education was given further praise in a study into pupil performance across 40 counties by the Organisation for Economic Cooperation and Development (OECD). 'Finland was the undisputed winner,' noted Warwick Mansell in the *TES* (6 May, 2005). Mansell went on to say: 'There is little setting or streaming. Even in subjects such as maths, where differences in pupils' capabilities can be great, the philosophy is to educate children in all-ability classrooms.'

This issue of there being wide differences in students' mathematical capabilities is one I suggest is the root cause behind decisions to create ability groups. Yet the preponderance to ignore the fact that all groups of pupils have wide variations of cognition and attainment in them is disingenuous. Give a class an accessible problem to work on, have loads of extension tasks sprinkled liberally around the classroom, find appropriate challenges, and we will find setting can be consigned to the dustbin of educational theory.

However, education has been the constant focus of both Labour and Conservative governments since Callaghan's Ruskin Lecture in 1976. The one-size-fits-all mantra was used to criticise the basis of comprehensive education. Furthermore, setting by ability was strongly encouraged by the 1997 Labour government: for example, in their White Paper, Excellence in Schools (July 1997), setting was advocated by the following: 'setting pupils according to ability … as one way of modernising the comprehensive principle'.

In 2000, in a leaked Labour Policy Forum document (*The Guardian*, 27 May, 2000), the following appeared: 'We want to see schools which focus on what works and abandon any residual dogmatic attachment to mixed-ability teaching.' This language of 'what works' seems to suggest a notion of 'common sense'. However, for thousands of children who experience a bottom-set curriculum and who consequently have bottom-set expectations placed upon them, setting may not necessarily feel to be something that 'works' or something that makes sense to them: Ollerton (2001) 'Support for Learning'.

However, there is, potentially, a saviour in our midst in the form of Ofsted. In the 2004 and 2005 subject study reports (into mathematics) the following quotes appear:

> *Too many pupils begin a course aimed at the foundation tier of entry for GCSE, which is limited in nature and ambition, rather than continuing with a broader teaching programme until a later decision about GCSE entry can be made (2004).*

> *Inflexible setting arrangements in Key Stage 4 lead many pupils to believe that their GCSE goals in mathematics are limited in nature and ambition. Many become disaffected and choose to channel their energy and enthusiasm into other subject areas in which they believe they will achieve better results (2005).*

Both quotes suggest a growing recognition that setting might not be all it is cracked up to be. If through inflexible setting arrangements we create a situation of significant numbers of students who write off their chances of achieving the holy grail of at least a grade C at GCSE, perhaps we should not be surprised if some of these students find other ways of gaining kudos. This can and does happen and leads to disillusionment, frequently manifested in poor behaviour and attendance, creating difficulties for teachers and fellow students alike.

As a Head of Department between 1986 and 1995 we operated a textbook-free, problem-solving, accessible-starting-point, extension-task curriculum model in mathematics. This meant we did not have to determine which tier of GCSE examination students would be entered for until such information had to be sent to the exam board. From February in Year 11 we practised going through past papers. Interestingly enough, and possibly because we had worked on developing students' personal responsibility, it was unproblematic to have students working on all three tiers of paper in the same lesson. Answers to the papers were freely available so students could identify personal targets and revision needs, and choose to seek help when necessary. In mixed-attainment groups Year 11 students quite naturally helped one another, having been encouraged to work in this way from the beginning of Year 7.

Given that teaching something is the most powerful way of learning something and deepening one's understanding of a process or of a concept, then having students teach each other is a fundamentally important strategy. Above all is the issue of students' dignity and self-esteem. If students in 'top' sets are sometimes referred to as 'the cream', what does this say about those in the 'bottom' set? Giving every student top-set learning opportunities, so all can experience mathematics in ways that enable them to do their best with what is on offer rather than some being offered a restricted mathematical diet, is fundamental to mixed-attainment grouping.

Teaching in mixed-ability groups ... 'Well, we wouldn't do it any other way!'

We developed a range of strategies and used a lot of equipment and problem-solving-based approaches to teach mathematics. We also had a lot of visitors. On one occasion a colleague was being quizzed during morning break by a group of visitors about how it was possible to teach mathematics in mixed-ability groups. His response was: 'Well, we wouldn't do it any other way!' At the time this was interesting because as a department we had evolved from teaching mathematics in setted groups to mixed groups, year by year, over a four-year period. Part of this process involved the use of fortnightly timetabled departmental meetings to share ideas for the classroom and to evaluate how our teaching in mixed groups was progressing. Subsequently, teaching in mixed groups became the most obvious and normal way to teach mathematics and, having started to develop a departmental pedagogy, we would not think about teaching any other way. We looked at starting points and discussed extension tasks, shared concerns and considered what was working well.

As such, we engaged in a massive amount of in-house professional and curriculum development. Working towards teaching in mixed groups was, therefore, the driving force behind many developments, where everything became connected: strategies, resources, schemes of work, methods of assessment, furniture arrangements, improvements in GCSE results and, by comparison to subjects taught in 'ability' groups, better-behaved students in our classrooms.

Difficulties with differentiation

The most common reason I hear for creating 'ability' groups is to minimise the ability range, thus enabling teachers to 'target' their teaching at an appropriate level and to 'sort out' difficulties with differentiation. Even in the most tightly setted group a range of attainment exists: in one school I visited, the 'lowest' set number went as far as 13. Just imagine being taught in set 13 out of 13. Working with differentiation is complex – but then so is teaching. To attempt to avoid wide variations of differentiation is to simplify what cannot be simplified: the complexity of teaching 30 individual children. If setting is used to try to make differentiation easier, then dangers exist of teaching primarily to a specific level. However, the notion of a level for a class does not exist – it never has done and never will do. Understanding is a moveable feast relating to individuals, not a set menu for a whole class.

In recent years there has been a significant drive by the now-defunct national strategy for mathematics and pressure from Ofsted (not unfortunately defunct!), for teachers to show they have prepared different levels of work for a class, usually operating at three levels. This is complete and utter garbage. How anyone can believe that levels of work they prepare can be matched to three different levels of ability within a class is puerile. Differentiated learning occurs at as many different levels in a classroom as there are learners in the class. Differentiated learning is also about the depth of cognition that occurs as a continuum by contrast to discrete or different categories. As such, using tasks that are ripe for extension that enable students to go to different depths of sense-making are ones that support learning per se.

I recently worked with a Year 2 class where the teacher asked me to prepare a lesson based upon understanding the idea of 'difference between'. What I did not need to know was what the in-class ability grouping was. This was because I decided we were going to do some people-mathematics. This involved each child and myself holding a number, written on a piece of card, from 1 to 22. I initially asked everyone to find another person who had a difference of 2 between their numbers. This created a situation where not everybody could find a partner (for example, if number 3 found number 5, then number 1 was left on her or his own). I then said 'Okay, now find all the people who have a difference of 2 with your number'. Before long two groups were formed ... perhaps you recognise this as one of the tasks described in Chapter 4. What was interesting is how the children realised they needed to stand in sequential orders, 1, 3, 5, 7 ... and 2, 4, 6, 8 ... We had a great time, calling out our numbers in loud voices, quiet voices, happy voices, singing voices, etc. Before long the class were forming three groups with a difference of 3, four groups with a difference of 4 – children were happily finding one another, the class teacher got busy with a camera and we all had a jolly time. As for working with so-called ability groups – well, I don't think so. Unsurprisingly, this was not necessary. Children were helping each other!

Planning lessons in ways that acknowledges and seeks to accommodate differentiation is at the heart of effective teaching and natural learning. As such it is imperative to look at methods of teaching that embrace differentiation rather than creating structural and organisational edifices to overcome difficulties with it. The issue in mixed-ability classrooms has nothing to do with minimising the range and has everything to do with maximising opportunities for working with students' differences ... and differences are normal.

Ways of working with groups of students with wide-ranging aspirations, motivations, current attainments and future achievements are:

1 Constructing modules or collections of ideas that offer students a fresh start.
2 Developing a range of teaching strategies.

A fresh start

I have already discussed in some detail the model of constructing modules based upon accessible, rich starting points, and devising a range of extension tasks. This model is based on helping individuals to find their own level in order to help them develop their mathematical thinking beyond their current level or comfort zone. A significant issue from students' perspectives is that each module offers a fresh-start opportunity. So, no matter what anyone has achieved in the past, anyone can achieve differently in the future.

This is the basis of inclusion and self-determination. 'Levels' do not need to be assigned to individual performance because, unremarkably, human nature does not countenance the notion that human beings operate at certain fixed or predicted levels. In reality, we shift between levels of cognition, sometimes failing to see the most obvious idea staring us in the face, while at other times making an intuitive leap and finding a solution to a problem when we least expected to.

On one occasion, I remember waking up in the middle of the night with the solution to a problem I had been working and getting stuck on for an Open University course. So vivid was the solution as I reached consciousness I had to write it down there and then in case the memory evaded me in the morning. This was certainly an amazing event: however, it confirmed to me the power of one's mind and its capability of operating at highly sophisticated levels even when the rest of the person lay sleeping.

Having a fresh start at the beginning of each module means past achievements do not predict future accomplishments. To help students realise their potential and develop their mathematical thinking, teachers need to develop a wide range of strategies. Access is the key. I align to the notion of a fresh start the phrase 'hope springs eternal' and, as a football fan, this phrase has a ring of truth – certainly as a fan in the Atatürk Olympic Stadium in 2005 with Liverpool 3–0 down to AC Milan at half-time. Fresh start or what!

Similarly, in YNWA classrooms, students must be encouraged to recognise they are never a 'lost cause' and how opportunities to achieve and to make sense of concepts that may initially appear insurmountable are always feasible. To help students work from such an optimistic perspective, they must be encouraged to inhabit mindsets of being able to overcome barriers to learning. Expectations of self and of their teachers play a significant part here; experiencing mathematics in classrooms that is not based upon students' measured ability is fundamental to raising self-worth.

Developing a range of teaching strategies

One of the more amazing features of our departmental shift towards teaching in mixed-ability groups was the wide range of strategies we developed to cater for different students' attainments. This did not mean we attempted to construct individual learning packages, nor did we use an individualised mathematics scheme based upon hundreds of workcards.

We did, however, amass many strategies and use a range of resources. To introduce a planned extension task for the first time during a module, I would temporarily gather together those students who I felt were, or soon would be, ready to work on a further idea, and work with this group for the next few minutes. Subsequently, as I sensed more students were ready to extend their thinking, I might ask a student who had already begun this task to temporarily take on the mantle of 'teacher'. Asking students to explain ideas to one another is both a valuable teaching resource and a powerful way of helping students consolidate through repetition and deepen their knowledge. If during a module one student became 'stuck', I would frequently suggest this person talk to another whom I was confident could provide help. An important aspect of this strategy was that it was not always higher-attaining, more confident students who helped their lower-attaining peers.

Sometimes quite the reverse happened. For example, on one occasion I asked a student who had a statement of special educational need (and who *loved* computers) to explain to a student destined for a high grade at GCSE (and who claimed to hate computers) how to use a dynamic geometry program. What was interesting about this particular event was the higher-attaining student recognised I had another agenda, which was about boosting the SEN student's self-esteem. She was absolutely right, and we both knew it!

Making use of paired-talk and feedback strategies and developing this way of working to groups of four students is a powerful strategy to support learning. Using people-math, where learners move away from behind their desks and become moveable pieces or numbers in puzzles, is another strategy. Getting students to prepare presentations where they explain something they have been working on is another powerful way of consolidating knowledge.

The important issue is utilising an eclectic mix of ways of organising learning so students are never quite sure about what their next mathematics lesson might be like. Keep 'em guessing, I say – reveal your objectives at the expense of students' interest and engagement. There's nowt like surprises.

The ebb and flow of an inclusive classroom

The rhythm of any lesson is very much one of ebb and flow. This is the stuff of classrooms. To recognise the web of relationships that exists between teacher, students and mathematics means using one's own relationships with mathematics and with students to help them forge a stronger, more confident relationship with mathematics. We do not need to label the high achievers and those who struggle: we will find this out quickly enough, but such perceptions cannot remain fixed. If we stick rigidly to any judgements we make and use this information to form different 'ability' groups, then we attribute ourselves with powers and responsibilities we have no right to claim.

There's a lovely quote from Bishop Desmond Tutu: 'Without all the colours there would be no rainbow.' To create a rainbow of achievement and provide opportunities for all children to become confident, to find ways of helping them all make sense of the most abstract discipline, to 'shine' mathematically, requires them to be included. The more the kids shine, the more we get out of our teaching. Finding ways of including everyone to learn mathematics without separation or segregation is to help everyone add up.

Postscript

I recently had the enormous pleasure of working in a primary school. I had been invited to bring some problem-solving ideas and to work with pupils across the Year 2 to Year 6 age range. Yet again I was reminded of the vibrant places primary schools are. I never cease to be amazed at the amount of nurturing that takes place within them, the hundreds of daily interactions that take place through to the fantastic displays that adorn classrooms, corridors and the school hall. This is not in any way a criticism of what happens in secondary schools. Once we throw adolescence into the teaching-and-learning mix then some things change in terms of managing classroom situations. However, a common issue that runs through education per se is the amount and degree of care teachers have for those they teach and how this caring is manifested moment by moment inside and outside classrooms. Each day in schools there will be many anecdotes that exemplify how teachers go well beyond what anyone would expect them to do to earn their pay cheques.

By going 'well beyond' I refer to the support teachers offer pupils to help them through difficulties, celebrate achievements and engage with their social and emotional development. The vast majority of teachers not only see this as part and parcel of the job – they also take professional pride in carrying out such roles.

Returning to my recent experience, one of the teachers, Jonathan, when describing his Year 5/6 class prior to my working with them, said: 'They're a lovely class and will appreciate having someone new coming in offering them something different to do.' His words could not have held greater truth. The rhythm of the classroom was wonderful as pupils worked on the main puzzle and later as some worked on developments of the task. The class felt to be in perfect harmony with their quietly spoken teacher as he quickly worked out what the task was all about and, therefore, how and to whom he might offer support.

After the lesson we talked about what place this kind of work, based upon problem-solving using the binary system, had to do with tests and league tables. How would the work the pupils did together with further development tasks they could continue to do in subsequent lessons help them in their Key Stage 2 national tests? We talked about how these tests fail to measure the emotional aspects of learning and how they fail to enhance pupils' creativity and problem-solving capabilities.

When we add up the pieces that frame all aspects of learning and development and therefore the fundamental roles schools play, I question how any school's results at Key Stage 2, Key Stage 4 and Key Stage 5 are anything more than a pitiable measure of what really goes on. These measurements are a complete and utter undervaluation of children's and, therefore, schools' real achievements. If the quality of education is to be recognised by both the immeasurable as well as the measurable it needs to be released from narrow, political shackles and from the stranglehold with which it is gripped. Schools are currently dominated by accountability and compliance upheld by inspection based upon flawed data and individual, unmoderated, subjective opinion. Consequently, two questions remain with me. The first is: who are these buggers that need to learn how to add up? My second is: when are these buggers going to be held to account due to their failure to add up?

Bibliography

ATM (1989) *Points of Departure 3*, Derby, Phelan Printers

Ashworth, K., (1995) *You need to use the calculator*, MicroMath Vol. 11 No 3, Derby, ATM

Ahmed, A., (Project Director) (1987) *Better Mathematics*, London, HMSO

Bloomfield, A., (1990) *People Maths*, Cheltenham, Stanley Thorne

Cockcroft, W., (1982) *Mathematics Counts:* Report into Inquiry into Teaching Mathematics in Schools, London, HMSO

Courant, R., and Robbins, H., (1941) *What is Mathematics*, Oxford University Press

Cundy, H., M., and Rollett, A., P., (1952) *Mathematical Models*, Oxford University Press

DES (1985) *HMI Mathematics from 5 to 16*, London, HMSO

Gattegno, C., (1963) *For the Teaching of Mathematics*, (Volume One), Great Britain, Lamport, Gilbert

Hart, S., Dixon, A., Drummond, M., J., and McIntyre (2004) *Learning without limits*, Maidenhead, Open University Press

HMI (2003) *Expecting the Unexpected: Developing Creativity in Primary and Secondary Schools*, Ofsted E-publication, reference HMI1612

—(2004) Ofsted Subject Reports 2002/03, *Mathematics in Secondary Schools*, www.ofsted.gov.uk

—(2005) Ofsted Subject Reports 2003/04, *Mathematics in Secondary Schools*, www.ofsted.gov.uk

Lacey, P., (1998) *Using Geometric Images of Number to Teach Mental Addition and Subtraction*, Mathematics Teaching 163, Derby, ATM

Bibliography

Mansell, W., (2005) *Reach for the Finnish line*, Times Educational Supplement

Moon, B., and Shelton-Mayes, A., (eds) (1994) *Teaching and learning in the secondary school*, London, Routledge

NCC, (1989) *Mathematics Non-Statutory guidance*, York, National Curriculum Council,

Ollerton, M., (2001) 'Inclusion and Entitlement, Equality of Opportunity and Quality of Curriculum Provision'. *Support for Learning* vol. 16. no. 1.

—(2002) *Learning and Teaching Mathematics Without a Textbook*, Derby, ATM

—(2004) *Creating positive classrooms*, London, Continuum

—(2005) *100 Ideas for Teaching Mathematics*, London, Continuum

Ollerton, M., and Watson, A., (2001) *Inclusive Mathematics 11–18*, London, Continuum

Pennac, D., (2010) *School Blues*, Quercus, & London, Maclehose Press

Pirsig, R., (1976) *Zen and the Art of Motorcycle Maintenance*, London, Corgi

Smith, A., (2004) *Making Mathematics Count*, London, Department for Education and Skil,ls,

Sotto, E., (1994) *When Teaching Becomes Learning: A Theory and Practice of Teaching*, London, Cassell

Sukhnandan, L., with Lee, B., (1998) *Streaming, Setting and Grouping by Ability: A Review of the Literature*, Slough, NFER

Sutcliffe, D (1989) *Partitioning Numbers*, MT 127, Derby, ATM

Watson, A., and Mason, M., (1998) *Questions and Prompts for Mathematical Thinking*, Derby, ATM

Wilby, P., (2005) *Little improvement in lot of the poor*, Times Educational Supplement

Index